100 Ideas for
Primary Teachers:

Supporting EAL Learners

Other titles in the 100 Ideas for Primary Teachers series:

100 Ideas for Primary Teachers:

Supporting EAL Learners

Chris Pim

BLOOMSBURY EDUCATION
LONDON OXFORD NEW YORK NEW DELHI SYDNEY

BLOOMSBURY EDUCATION
Bloomsbury Publishing Plc
50 Bedford Square, London, WC1B 3DP, UK

BLOOMSBURY, BLOOMSBURY EDUCATION and
the Diana logo are trademarks of Bloomsbury Publishing Plc

First published in Great Britain, 2018 by Bloomsbury Education

A catalogue record for this book is available from the British Library

ISBN: PB: 978-1-4729-4647-8; ePDF: 978-1-4729-4648-5;
ePub: 978-1-4729-4645-4

2 4 6 8 10 9 7 5 3 1

Typeset by Newgen KnowledgeWorks Pvt. Ltd., Chennai, India
Printed and bound by CPI Group (UK) Ltd., Croydon, CR0 4YY

MIX
Paper from
responsible sources
FSC® C013604

All papers used by Bloomsbury Publishing Plc are natural, recyclable products
from wood grown in well managed forests. The manufacturing processes
conform to the environmental regulations of the country of origin.

To find out more about our authors and books visit
www.bloomsbury.com and sign up for our newsletters.

Contents

Acknowledgements

My deepest thanks to Astrid Dinneen for her diligence in proofreading the manuscript and for her insightful suggestions for new ideas and advice on how to improve the organisation of the content. I also wish to thank these other professionals: Catherine Driver (EAL proficiency stages and assessment frameworks, BICS and CALP, Cummins' framework, Comprehensible input, Miscue analysis, Word building and Morphology), Babette Brown (Persona dolls), Clare Reed (TalkingPartners@Primary), Julie Spencer (Talking Maths), Clare Williams (Drama), Astrid Dinneen (the Young Interpreter Scheme®).

Introduction

In many ways, effective provision for pupils learning English as an additional language (EAL) is very straightforward. Ensuring pupils are safe and settled, engaging effectively with families and providing high quality teaching are all key principles. But it is also true that most EAL learners have an additional set of complex needs related to their distinct social, cultural, religious and linguistic contexts. EAL learners are not a homogenous group; their only common factor is that their first language is not English. Many EAL learners come from stable academic backgrounds; they may speak and write a number of different languages and may eventually outperform their monolingual peers. Others have more complex histories, coming from less stable backgrounds and with fragmented previous education. They may have limited literacy in their first language and have undiagnosed additional needs – their achievement will be less predictable and will require a range of extra support and interventions.

All EAL learners have the benefit of one or more languages beyond English and benefit enormously when they develop age-appropriate (or better) literacy in at least their first language (L1) – the language they grew up with or were influenced by at an early age. This is an important principle to recognise and build upon in school. Practitioners will also need to consider the social, cultural and religious contexts of their pupils' lives and how this affects their sense of identity. These important aspects can be addressed through strong leadership, effective whole-school provisioning and outreach to the family and wider community.

In the United Kingdom, the accepted position regarding EAL teaching and learning is that pupils best acquire English within the context of the curriculum. It is generally true that what is good practice for EAL learners will be good practice for all.

As a simple ready-reckoner, it can sometimes be helpful to use a set of well-established terms to talk about pupils and where they are in their acquisition of English. These terms are not linked to assessment and data. They are connected with how long a pupil has been learning English and what research and experience tells us about how long, on average, it might take to acquire English for a range of purposes across the curriculum. Therefore, in my description of how the 100 ideas in this book relate to children at different stages in their acquisition of English, I make specific reference to three 'groups':

- **New-to-English learners** – either children entering Reception or new arrivals to the United Kingdom, these pupils are at the earliest stages of learning English. With appropriate support, these pupils will make rapid progress in the early stages of acquiring colloquial language and in their engagement with the more academic nature of the curriculum.
- **Beginner EAL learners** – learners who either have acquired some English in their country of origin or have been studying for two to four years in the United Kingdom. Towards the end of a two-year period, they are likely to exhibit reasonable oral skills and may have just started to read and write independently.
- **Advanced EAL learners** – those who either have had extensive English teaching abroad, perhaps in English-medium schools, or have been studying English for several years in the United Kingdom. These learners will generally have well-developed oral skills, will be beginning to read and write competently and will eventually reach, or in many cases exceed, the attainment level of their monolingual peers across the curriculum. However, we know that some advanced learners plateau at particular points in their education and often require specific types of classroom teaching to move them on in their learning.

About this book

This book will be essential reading for students on initial teacher training programmes as well as for more experienced practitioners working as teachers, TAs or in other support roles in the school.

This second edition has been completely updated and rewritten specifically for a primary phase audience. Some of the original ideas have been removed and been repurposed for a secondary version – *100 Ideas for Secondary Teachers: Supporting EAL Learners.* This primary version also features more than 15 brand-new ideas.

The 100 ideas contained within these pages aim to be both practical and simple to implement. At the same time, each idea represents a challenge to the reader. It may reinforce already-held beliefs, giving confidence in the support you already offer to EAL learners and encouraging you to take provision to the next stage. It may, however, require an adjustment in your thinking, resulting in alternative approaches around school and in the classroom. Finally, I hope that each idea has been articulated so succinctly that it will be obvious to you what further action needs to be taken in your specific context to bring the idea to fruition.

As you will see, the book has been organised into different sections. The earlier sections deal with the very real challenge of how to settle, assess and provide for new pupils, especially those newly arrived from abroad. The middle sections focus on effective teaching and learning and specifically how to develop speaking, listening, reading and writing across the curriculum. The key sections towards the end of the book illustrate how important it is to take a holistic view of catering for the needs of EAL learners, where effective whole-school provision involves all staff whatever their particular role in the school. Senior leaders, such as the Ethnic Minority Achievement (EMA)/EAL coordinator, will find these later sections particularly useful in understanding how to reach out to the wider community, work more effectively with parents and develop whole-school approaches that truly enable all EAL learners to reach their full potential.

Chris Pim

Acronyms

AfL	Assessment for Learning
BICS	Basic Interpersonal Communication Skill
BAME	Black and Minority Ethnic (also known as BME)
CALP	Cognitive Academic Language Proficiency
CPD	Continuing Professional Development
DARTs	Directed Activities Related to Texts
EAL	English as an Additional Language
EMA	Ethnic Minority Achievement
ESL	English as a Second Language
ILP	Individual Language Plan
IWB	Interactive Whiteboard
KWL	What I Know, What I Want to Know, What I Have Learned
LSA	Learning Support Assistant
L1	First Language
L2	Second Language
NALDIC	National Association for Language Development in the Curriculum
NEN	National Education Network
SEND	Special Educational Needs and Disability
TA	Teaching Assistant
VC	Videoconference
WBRI	White British

How to use this book

This book includes quick, easy and practical ideas for you to dip in and out of, to help you provide the best support possible for EAL learners in the primary classroom.

Each idea includes:

- a catchy title, easy to refer to and share with your colleagues
- an interesting quote linked to the idea
- a summary of the idea in bold, making it easy to flick through the book and identify an idea you want to use at a glance
- a step-by-step guide to implementing an idea.

Each idea also includes one or more of the following:

Teaching tip

Practical tips and advice for how and how not to run the activity or put the idea into practice.

Taking it further

Ideas and advice for how to extend the idea or develop it further.

Bonus idea ★

There are 52 bonus ideas in this book that are extra exciting, extra original and extra interesting.

Share how you use these ideas and find out what other practitioners have done using **#100ideas**.

Induction and transition

Part 1

School information and induction materials

'Past experience tells me that newly-arrived families from black and minority ethnic backgrounds often face linguistic and cultural barriers that can inhibit full access to school-based information.'

Ensuring that information is as accessible as possible can avoid embarrassing mistakes and pre-empt common assumptions that parents may have because of their own past educational experiences in their country of origin. The additional cost associated with customising websites and induction booklets will be well worth it in the long run.

Teaching tip

For many years, the school pupil annual census has asked schools to collect data about *ethnicity*. As of 2016 schools are also required to collect data on the *English language proficiency* (Idea 12) of their EAL pupils. Additionally, the census asks questions about *nationality* and *country of birth*. It is very important that the school makes clear that this additional information is completely optional and parents are under no obligation to provide it if they don't want to.

Many schools produce general information booklets and induction materials for new-arrival families, whatever their background or L1. If this information is available at your school, adapt these materials further to reflect the major ethnic groups within the local community and to help cater for the needs of families that have recently arrived from abroad.

Where possible, try to translate the most important elements of the information available, although this may only be viable for the larger minority groups within the school. Bear in mind that some parents or carers are not fully literate in their L1 and so will not be able to access written translations.

Families who are new to the United Kingdom may have very little understanding of school processes in this country, and while we should be cautious about making generalisations, it can be useful to clearly state the school's position on various matters:

- Explain that all learners have to 'study' the full National Curriculum as well as stating the school's position on typically occurring issues such as religious education and worship and sex and relationships education.

- Offer clear guidance on homework for each year group (since some families traditionally expect more than the recommended amount).
- Be clear about the legalities around attendance and how this might impact families who choose to take an extended family visit to their home country.
- Extend a clear invitation for families to be fully involved in all aspects of school life – sometimes parents lack confidence to do so. Usually parents are keen to get involved, but in some countries parents don't traditionally have much contact with their child's school.
- Provide clear explanations of what it means to have special educational needs and disabilities, as some parents or carers find this 'diagnosis' hard to accept for their child.
- Explain the importance of accurately recording their child's ethnicity and language on the admissions form.

Taking it further

It might be a good idea to release school information through bilingual podcasts and videos hosted on the school's website.

Effective parent conferencing

'Many parents feel intimidated by schools and this can be especially true for those new to the country and in situations where they are not fully proficient in English.'

The initial meeting with a family can be a seminal moment in their child's education and it is vital that schools find out what special arrangements may be required to ensure a positive first experience and facilitate a strong relationship in the longer term.

Where possible, meeting with the parents or carers of a newly-arrived EAL learner in order to obtain important background information can be extremely beneficial. Here are some tips to help you to prepare for a parent conference:

- Invite all parents or carers and the target learner to the meeting; let them know the focus of the meeting and its intended length in advance.
- Letters should be followed up with phone calls; use the child's L1 where possible.
- When an interpreter is necessary, arrange for one to be present during the meeting. Brief interpreters before the meeting, and provide them with copies of paperwork such as school induction forms and questionnaires in advance.
- Be flexible about timing, as both parents may work. Note that in some Muslim families a male adult may need to accompany the mother or female carer.

At the meeting:

- Be aware that greeting customs can vary across cultures, and some adults may choose not to shake hands upon first meeting.
- Seating should be arranged informally.

Bonus idea ★

Many new families do not have access to a typical support network from friends and family and often have childcare requirements. Offering a crèche facility or providing a school-based adult to look after a baby/toddler during the meeting is a beneficial strategy.

- When an interpreter is involved, always try to direct questions to the family members, maintain eye contact and gesture liberally to reinforce meaning.
- Work through a set of prepared questions, and make notes as the meeting progresses; it can help to explain that the information will be confidential to the school, except where there is a required child-protection disclosure.
- Ensure that there is ample opportunity for the parents or carers to ask any immediate questions about the school.

At the end of the meeting, establish a review date with parents or carers to provide feedback as to how their child has settled in at the school.

IDEA 3

Gathering background information

'EAL learners are not a homogenous group; the only factor that unites them is that English is not their first language. Therefore, without additional knowledge, making general assumptions about them should be avoided.'

In order to inform best practice and provision for each individual learner, schools need to collect as much information as possible. Parents/carers, alongside their children, are an integral part of this process.

As previously mentioned, it is important to gather background information about newly-arrived learners as soon as possible after they start school. Try to capture details about previous schooling — for example, what subjects have or have not been studied. Find out about general aptitude, proficiency in L1 and other languages, and pertinent medical, social and cultural issues. Other useful evidence includes achievement in public examinations, reports and samples of work from the country of origin. All this information will help you to develop an effective induction programme and to consider the most appropriate teaching and learning provision, including setting/grouping arrangements (Idea 17) and other critical decisions.

You will be able to obtain much of this information at a parent conference (Idea 2) although sometimes this is not possible because children arrive as unaccompanied minors. At other times, lengthy communication is not possible because parents or carers have limited English and securing the services of an interpreter is not possible, but every little helps!

> **Bonus idea** ★
>
> Some schools use a free online background information collation tool to support this process. Such a tool presents a series of typical questions through an online form, supported through L1 audio files. While responses are mainly made through tick boxes and writing is kept to a minimum, it is recommended that a teacher/TA facilitates the use of the tool. Once complete, the system produces a written report in English that can be printed or saved and incorporated into a wider early profile. For more information, see: newarrivals.segfl.org.uk.

Survival language

'Being able to use a few words and phrases in a new language can give new arrivals a tremendous amount of confidence, particularly with communicating basic needs.'

Survival language is not something you should specifically teach, particularly at the expense of mainstream teaching. This type of language will be learned naturally through pupil interaction and bespoke resources provided by you or another practitioner.

Build up a range of 'survival language' materials to support those new to English. This will help them settle more easily and enhance their interaction with adults and peers. Survival language introduces learners to essential vocabulary and simple phrases, e.g. greetings, numbers, colours, time-based nouns, everyday objects and imperatives. Common questions are also useful, e.g. 'May I go to the toilet?'

Basic language is best supported with familiar imagery, emoticons and emojis to help convey meaning. Visual timetables (Idea 6), vocabulary fans, booklets and wall displays are all great for packaging up survival language for EAL learners. Learners literate in L1 will benefit from having dual-language versions to aid knowledge-transfer between languages. These learners should also be encouraged to keep a record of new language as it is encountered.

Remember, survival language is not something that needs to be specifically taught, especially if it takes time out of the curriculum. It is intended to support learners both in and out of the classroom during their first few weeks at a new school and can be given out in a pack when they arrive. It is also important not to demean learners with inappropriate materials; older learners will appreciate materials that are relatively sophisticated and supported by imagery with a more adult feel.

Taking it further

There are many free online resources available for survival language, such as this survival language vocabulary fan: http://wsh.wokingham. gov.uk/EasySiteWeb/ GatewayLink. aspx?alId=233433.

Bonus idea ★

Emojis are a great way to convey simple ideas. They are easy to incorporate into texts as phones/tablets often have an emoji set on the soft keyboard. There are also numerous free emojis available online.

Language audit

'The most effective practitioners know which languages are most commonly used within their school community. They make the effort to find out about how different languages work and use this knowledge to enhance teaching and learning.'

Conducting an audit of language use among the whole school community is a useful first step in terms of preparing for new arrivals.

Finding out about the languages used within the school community really helps schools develop the most effective provision for EAL learners and their families; this is important for new arrivals as well as EAL learners who were born in the United Kingdom. Good practice suggests that schools should gather information about the breadth of languages used by learners and their parents or carers, and should enter the information onto their assessment systems.

Here are some points for consideration:

- When new-arrival EAL learners and their families first encounter the school education system, they will feel more welcome if they get the sense that their background has been taken into consideration. When an interpreter is required, having one present at a parent conference (Idea 2) will help you gather critical background information.
- Class-based practitioners should prepare their classroom and their class for a new arrival by learning a few words in the EAL learner's L1, preparing relevant displays and gathering useful resources, including dual-language dictionaries.

- Finding out about the features of specific languages helps with L1 assessments (Idea 13), as well as in understanding how speaking and writing another language can impact upon how an EAL learner begins to speak and write in English. Features to consider include the written script, writing directionality, punctuation, word order and numeric symbols, among others.
- Learning about other languages gives practitioners confidence to capitalise on the linguistic knowledge and skills of their learners as inspiration for embedding intercultural work within the curriculum, such as language tasters, number systems and numerical methods from around the world. (See Part 8 for more information on this.)
- Many learners will continue to learn their L1 at home, at community language schools (Idea 87) or both. EAL learners will appreciate schools that routinely celebrate their achievements in L1.

> **Bonus idea** ★
>
> Why not celebrate the additional languages that children can speak by using them in a school assembly? Those attending a supplementary language school sometimes gain certificates which could be presented during an assembly.

Visual timetables

'Sometimes the simplest resource can make a world of difference to a new arrival who is struggling to adjust to their new learning context.'

Visual timetables provide language-free reassurance to children at the beginning of their school day and can be instantly referred to whenever a child needs to know what activity is coming up next.

Taking it further

Produce sound-enabled versions, in English and/ or other languages to add further information. Simple approaches might include a daily planner with information recorded on *talking tins*; a weekly planner laid out in the pages of a *talking photo album* with associated recordings; or a printed timetable with talking stickers and recordings made with Mantra Lingua's *PENpal*™ (Idea 57).

School structures and routines can require a huge adjustment for younger EAL learners when they first start school, as well as for those newly arrived from abroad. Some new-arrival learners are unused to rigid timetables, while others may find it hard to understand the notion of free choice in learning. Visual timetables are a simple, practical way of tangibly presenting the abstract idea of time; they also help to reinforce the organisation of events on a daily basis.

As a talking point, try displaying a large visual timetable containing movable pictures of activities at the front of the class each morning. As activities change throughout the day, pictures can be moved around; doing so helps EAL learners know which activities are in progress and what will be coming later.

Individual versions can also be useful. When there is a free choice, such as deciding on activities for 'golden time', learners can self-determine which activities they want to tackle and in which order. It can also act as a focus of discussion between children and their parents or carers about what the child has done at school that day.

Develop a peer buddy programme

'I often use peers to support EAL learners who are new to the school, as they can help to explain school routines and offer friendship at breaks and lunchtimes.'

Not all peers will make suitable buddies for new-arrival EAL learners; buddies need to be confident, articulate communicators. While they do not need to be bilingual, sharing a strong first language with a child who is an early user of English can be a tremendous advantage.

It is a good idea to allocate a 'peer buddy' to any new-arrival EAL learner first starting school. Having a pool of potential buddies who can take turns to be with the new arrival on a daily basis will help ensure that no individual is overburdened. Potential buddies should be self-assured, trusted to model good behaviour and be confident English speakers. Peers who share a language with the new learner can act as interpreters or translators, which is particularly important for learners who are new to English.

All buddies should undergo basic training to help them understand the requirements of the role. Buddies can support EAL learners both in and out of lessons in a number of important ways. They can help explain school routines and act as advocates for the new learner, ensuring they remain safe throughout the day. They can also support the new learner in lessons by clarifying tasks and modelling good use of English across the curriculum.

A well-thought-out programme will benefit everyone. New arrivals will feel supported, while buddies learn from training and the opportunity to take on varied responsibilities. When the support finishes, certificates can be awarded in recognition of buddies' efforts.

Taking it further

The Young Interpreter Scheme® (Idea 97) takes peer buddying to a new level, with online training materials available to skill up a team of pupils to act as helpers for new arrivals and their families. Find out more here: http://emtas. hias.hants.gov.uk/course/ view.php?id=30.

Personal workbooks

'Stefan loves his new workbook. He says it makes him feel special and helps him keep on top of all the new things he encounters each day.'

Workbooks can be used in many different ways depending on a learner's background and level of literacy in English.

Provide new-arrival learners with a good-quality workbook which can be personalised. Workbooks may also contain useful resources provided by the school, such as a visual timetable (Idea 6) and survival vocabulary (Idea 4). Include academic keywords from different subjects, maps of the world and/or the UK and a basic history timeline. A set of thumbs-up/horizontal/down or red/amber/green traffic light cards can be useful visual tools for learners to show their level of understanding during class work.

All learners will benefit from using a workbook to record new vocabulary and writing in L1 and English. It can also serve as a homework communication tool for sending messages between home and school.

More advanced learners can use the workbook as a 'dialogue' journal to enter into a pictorial or written conversation with the class teacher. Less literate learners might start with drawings and simple annotations, and more confident writers might produce extensive prose.

Learners should use their dialogue journal to communicate things that are important to them, especially things unrelated to the curriculum. Since meaning is more important than correct form and spelling, it helps if the dialogue partner avoids correcting anything and responds in a similar informal style. Adult respondents may like to ask a key question, but their contribution will usually involve observational comments about what has been written, with the occasional follow-up question to keep the conversation moving.

Using *Google Earth*™ to help settle new arrivals

'Talking about something as familiar as "home" can be the one thing that encourages a child to start communicating.'

While most children will be more than happy to talk about their previous life in their home country, bear in mind that occasionally some children may not want to, having had a traumatic past or simply because they are very homesick.

Sometimes EAL learners are disorientated when they first come to live in the UK. They may find adjusting to another culture and a new home and settling in at school confusing and isolating. They may be unaware of where the UK is in relation to their home country, where their locality lies within the UK and even where their present home is in relation to the school. This activity works well in a one-on-one situation. Start off by asking where the learner used to live, e.g. 'Bangladesh'. In *Google Earth*™, show the revolving world and then beam down to the relevant country. Use the zoom, pan and tilt tools or keywords to find a locality that the learner recognises, identifying major features. Click on photographs as they appear, which will generate opportunities for conversation around familiar objects in a natural context.

Return to the UK, tracing the learner's route from their home country where possible.

Zoom down to the area of the learner's new home, noting major features on the way; it can be motivating to use the postcode to zoom right down on top of the house where the learner now lives. A walk around the area could also be made in *Google Streetview*™.

Taking it further

Encourage new arrivals to make an identity text (Idea 43) about their country of origin(s) using printed/digital maps and images taken from *Google Earth*™. These could be made into a scrapbook or even a talking book (Idea 44) with a voiceover in L1 and/or English.

Bonus idea ★

Google Streetview™ can now be browsed in 3D using a mobile phone and VR headset/*Google Cardboard*.

Using *Google Maps™/Earth™* to teach about locality

'I am constantly amazed at how little some new arrivals know about their new situation.'

Maps are a great way to visually show the relationship between different places in the locality and provide the opportunity to introduce all kinds of new vocabulary to a new EAL learner.

Google Maps™ (as well as *Google Earth™*) is a fantastic tool for showing geographical locality, the relationship between places, distances, directions and points of interest. Type in the postcode of a locality such as the learner's home or school. Zoom out a little to show the learner's home in relation to the school. Use the 'get directions' tool to plot a route from home to school and talk through the directions. Compare the routes for car and foot journeys. Now ask the learner to describe their actual journey to school using the visual support of roads and other features along the route.

Google Streetview™ allows a route to be traced by clicking through real photographs of an area. It's also possible to have a split view to see both map and Streetview™ at the same time. This is perfect for developing geographical vocabulary, locative prepositions, time-based cohesive devices and so on. Type keywords into the search bar to identify points of interest, such as 'college', 'park' or 'cinema'. Local places matching the keyword will be displayed on the map for further investigation.

Google Maps™ also support the development of map skills. Switching between 'map view' and 'satellite view' shows how maps diagrammatically relate to actual geographical features, while the distance-measurement tool shows how far apart places are and reinforces map scales.

Bonus idea ★

It is possible to make interactive tours for *Google Earth™* about any subject; these are called *Google Lit Trips*. A *Google Lit Trip* consists of a set of clickable map markers that overlay the map and contain text and graphics/video; each marker links to the next in a 'programmed' sequence. Try making an interactive tour for pupils/parents of the locality, showing off the major landmarks, and make it freely available via the school website.

Assessment, observation and planning

Part 2

Finding and using bilingual help

'It is impossible to overstate the value of having interpreters to help us understand the background and needs of our new-arrival EAL learners.'

Depending on the context and the level of confidentiality required, interpreters can range from formally trained professionals to members of staff and other adults within the community. For very informal situations, it can be appropriate to use articulate older pupils.

Taking it further

Interpreting and translation need to be integral parts of a school's support mechanism. Should it prove impossible to find appropriate help within the community and local authority, you may need to look farther afield. For example, most areas provide phone lines and interpreting/ translation services for a set fee depending on requirements. As a last resort, you could try *LanguageLine Solutions*®, a national interpreting and translation service, though this can be costly.

Bilingual helpers will ordinarily be peripatetic or school-based practitioners, but don't underestimate the role that parents can have. It is therefore a good idea to perform an audit on the whole school community to identify who can speak, read and write different languages and with what level of proficiency. An informal chat involves a different level of language proficiency and maturity than a formal assessment, which requires an individual to have good L1 proficiency and a full understanding of the need to be confidential.

Suitably qualified adult interpreters/translators will be useful for:

- parent conferencing (Idea 2) in order to gather critical background information on a new arrival
- formal assessment of a pupil's proficiency in L1 (Idea 13) to gain a realistic picture of the learner's proficiencies in other languages
- meeting parents – they may be more likely to attend with an interpreter present
- interpreting legal information around SEND
- meetings where there are potential child protection/safeguarding issues
- providing contextual information related to a child's background, e.g. religious/cultural factors and knowledge about different education systems around the world.

EAL proficiency stages – snapshot assessment

'The EAL proficiency stages are such a useful snapshot for all teachers.'

The use of standard EAL proficiency codes across England and Wales makes it easier for all teachers to plan support and differentiation for EAL learners at different stages.

In 2017, for the first time, the Department for Education required all schools to assign EAL proficiency stages to pupils who speak another language at home and in the community. This data must now be submitted in the School Census every January.

It is important for schools to give the responsibility for assigning the codes to a teacher, rather than a data manager. In most cases, the class teacher will be able to assign a 'best-fit' code (see below). The codes are designed to be applied across the curriculum rather than on the basis of what a child can/cannot do in English only.

The EAL proficiency data collected should enable schools to plan and make provision for EAL pupils at different stages of development. Be aware that these codes are not appropriate for tracking pupil progress as most children will move through codes A and B relatively quickly but then remain within codes C and D for lengthy periods of time. In order to track progress, schools will need to utilise an EAL assessment framework that is much more granular in detail (Idea 14).

The EAL proficiency stages are as follows:
   A – New to English
   B – Early acquisition
   C – Developing competence
   D – Competent
   E – Fluent.

Teaching tip

You may not need to submit data in January for international new arrivals starting school during and after October of the previous year. This is because they will not have not had enough time to fully settle and you are unlikely to have had time to gather enough information to inform a valid and robust judgement.

Taking it further

Visit www.gov.uk/government/publications/school-census-2016-to-2017-guide-for-schools-and-las for more information about the stages, including a detailed description of what each stage means and what it may look like in practice.

Assessing proficiency with languages other than English

'Knowing that an EAL learner has age-appropriate literacy or better in their first language tells us a lot about their previous schooling and their all-round aptitude for learning.'

While having access to an interpreter/translator will make a first language assessment easier, it is still possible to glean a lot of information without one.

It is really useful to know about the full language repertoire of everyone within the school community. For new-arrival EAL learners, an accurate assessment of proficiency in their L1, as well as other influencing languages, will help build a more complete picture of their general ability. Relevant information should include the following:

- the language considered to be L1, as well as all other languages used
- how long each language has been studied and when and for what purpose is it used
- proficiency in speaking, listening, reading and writing L1.

A rigorous assessment of L1 is best achieved in collaboration with speakers of the same language, particularly adults with an academic background, as they should be able to establish whether the learner is functioning at an age-appropriate level. Sometimes it is not possible to secure the services of a trained bilingual practitioner; it may be necessary to seek help from a parent or other adult, although impartiality and personal privacy should always be guaranteed in such cases.

School-based practitioners should not be dissuaded from assessing a child's L1 simply because bilingual support is unavailable at the

> **Taking it further**
>
> Hampshire EMTAS have produced a comprehensive e-learning guide to L1 assessment. Using video case studies, the unit details how to conduct an L1 assessment without the involvement of an adult L1 speaker. See here for details: http:// emtas.hias.hants.gov.uk/ course/view.php?id=19.

time. Moreover, many significant details of L1 proficiency can be ascertained by any skilled practitioner.

An L1 assessment without the presence of an L1 user might include the following:

Bonus idea ★

Record conversations or readings and scan samples of writing as these can always be reviewed by an L1 user at a later date.

Speaking and listening
- Watch an informal conversation between peers who share the same first language and look out for fluency, eye contact, body language, child-initiated conversation, etc.
- Ask the pupil to listen to two-way dialogue such as a podcast or TV programme and ask simple questions in English about what the child has heard.
- Play a sample of audio from a talking book and ask simple questions in English about what the child has heard.

Reading
- Listen to a learner read from a familiar, age-appropriate text – take note of pace, intonation and self-correction.
- Encourage the pupil to point as they read so that you can follow along, matching the text to what is being read.
- Watch for wider reading strategies such as using pictures to understand plot and make predictions.
- Where possible, check whether the learner is reading for meaning by asking simple questions in English.

Writing
- Obtain a piece of writing about a familiar story, setting or situation; consider overall length, handwriting, punctuation, demarcation and evidence of self-correction.

EAL assessment frameworks – ongoing formative assessment

'Salim was silent for several months before he spoke at all. Then his language developed rapidly for a year. I was surprised about the unevenness of it all.'

EAL learners tend to have spiky profiles of attainment across the curriculum, being able to demonstrate learning more easily in some subjects than others.

Taking it further

Several reputable academic organisations have published comprehensive EAL assessment frameworks that enable specialist teachers to record a baseline and assess termly progress as well as setting targets for future development. These can be accessed from the websites below.

NASSEA Framework – www.nassea.org.uk/eal-assessment-framework

Bell Foundation EAL Assessment – www.bell-foundation.org.uk/eal-programme.

After a few weeks settling in, an in-depth baseline assessment of language development should be conducted, ideally by the class teacher, and perhaps an EAL coordinator, using a comprehensive framework of 'can do' statements rather than a pen and paper (or online) test. Screening tests should also be avoided as they are standardised on the monolingual population.

The most valuable form of assessment is talking to and observing EAL learners doing tasks in a range of contexts. For the necessary ongoing assessment, the process should be repeated a minimum of twice a year. There is no national, statutory EAL assessment framework across all UK regions. Northern Ireland uses a system based on the Common European Framework of Reference for Languages (CEFR), but the rest of the UK use locally-based systems for recording progress.

A good EAL assessment framework should:

- show progress from beginner to fluent across the four language skills
- ideally, dovetail with the EAL fluency scale data captured for the annual census (Idea 12)
- include a focus on viewing as well as traditional reading skills to reflect the multimodal nature of our digital world.

EAL or SEND?

'When EAL learners fail to make adequate progress, it can be extremely difficult to unpick whether this is solely related to language/culture or if there may be an additional underlying SEND.'

It is important not to jump to conclusions. Take the time to gather information from as wide a range of people as possible, including from parents, practitioners and, potentially, health professionals.

While most EAL learners don't have an underlying SEND, it's evident that some do. However, experience suggests that when learners are experiencing problems at school, attributing difficulties to an underlying SEND is usually not the most relevant of starting points. First, don't rely on formal tests or screening programmes, as these are generally standardised on a monolingual population, and don't take potential linguistic and cultural barriers into account. Even non-verbal tests have inherent bias that can depress scores. Don't carry out any 'formal' assessment until learners have been well settled in the school for several weeks. It is important to gather a range of evidence to help inform any decisions, such as:

- information from parents or carers about their child's early childhood and previous educational experience
- observation of learners both in and out of class
- assessment of L1 proficiency (Idea 13)
- book scrutiny across a range of subjects
- analysis of English proficiency and progress over time (it is quite usual for EAL learners to have an uneven profile of achievement across the curriculum).

Take a diagnostic approach, and ask questions about all aspects of a learner's experience. Filter out irrelevant information and focus on factors that can't be explained by things like medical issues, fragmented education, language, culture or a traumatic past.

Teaching tip

When in doubt, seek advice from trained specialists in this area.

Taking it further

Hampshire Ethnic Minority and Traveller Achievement Service (EMTAS) has an extensive range of online EAL e-learning, including a comprehensive unit on distinguishing the difference between SEND and EAL: http://emtas.hias.hants.gov.uk/course/view.php?id=19.

Identifying able or high-potential learners

'When Grace arrived in our school she spoke no English, but her maths ability was exceptional. She made rapid progress in speaking and listening and was soon confident in French as well as English.'

Identifying talent and potential in EAL learners is quite easy. They often shine in mathematics or practical subjects and their progress in learning English is rapid.

Teaching tip

Able EAL learners will benefit from particular approaches that have been shown to accelerate achievement across the curriculum. Check out the Realising Equality and Achievement for Learners (REAL) website from London Gifted and Talented: www.realproject.org.uk.

Good practice suggests that the identification of able EAL (and BAME) learners should be broadly in line with that of the WBRI population. Consider these questions when EAL learners are under-represented in the able learners group:

- What might be the implications of an under-representation?
- What criteria do the school use to identify able learners?
- Are the criteria flexible enough to ensure fair opportunities to identify BAME/EAL learners, particularly those new to English?

Ensure able EAL learners are given equal access to the same enrichment opportunities as others, and celebrate their achievements.

Here are some additional ideas that may be particularly pertinent to bilingual pupils:

- use EAL learners with strong L1 skills as peer buddies for new arrivals (Idea 7);
- consider training pupils via The Young Interpreter Scheme® (Idea 97)
- display samples of writing in L1 alongside equivalent samples in English
- encourage learners to offer L1 taster classes for their peers
- celebrate the L1 learning achievements of EAL learners at supplementary language schools (Idea 87).

How to group EAL learners

'This work is too easy. I have already done it. I am getting bored.'

Self-esteem, motivation, progress and even behaviour can be adversely affected if learners are inappropriately grouped with 'less able' peers. EAL learners will benefit from being surrounded by articulate speakers who implicitly understand how best to act as a supportive classroom buddy.

Making the right decisions about grouping and setting is essential for all EAL learners to reach their full potential. Generally, EAL learners should be grouped according to academic potential rather than current English proficiency. A curriculum that matches the cognitive ability of the learner will build upon existing skills, maintain motivation and raise self-esteem. EAL learners benefit from effective use of language across the curriculum being modelled by orally proficient English speakers. In class discussions, offer EAL learners the opportunity to rehearse their ideas with a supportive peer before answering in front of the class. In a larger group, EAL learners will appreciate hearing a two-way conversation between confident English speakers. When using computers, try not to isolate EAL learners; instead, pair them with a good-language role model. Pairing same-language speakers together allows them to converse and think through ideas in a familiar language, which can really benefit learners, particularly those newer to English. As learners become more orally proficient, they will naturally begin to convert their thoughts into English, allowing them to participate confidently in conversation ahead of more formal oral and written tasks. Finally, take a flexible approach to the physical placement of EAL learners within the room. They should have a clear view of the board and be close to the class teacher – without being isolated or made to feel conspicuous.

Teaching tip

Don't assume that the most supportive strategy will be to provide adult support for beginner EAL learners, particularly if this means that they are seated with 'weaker' learners because that is where the class TA/other adult currently works. It is also imperative that TAs and other adults who occasionally 'support' EAL learners are properly trained in order to ensure that they don't employ approaches that are more suited to children with SEND, rather than tried-and-tested EAL strategies.

Withdrawal intervention

'They just want to be with their friends and treated the same as everyone else. Withdrawing them from class just isolates them further.'

In general, it is much harder to create a meaningful context for learning outside of the mainstream classroom. Moreover, the opportunity to create dynamic oral interaction is greatly reduced in one-to-one scenarios or where all the children are at an early stage of learning EAL.

Teaching tip

In general, withdrawal intervention is much more appropriate for advanced EAL learners than those who are newer to English. This is because advanced learners are more orally proficient in terms of colloquial language and are much better at articulating their strengths and weaknesses in terms of curriculum knowledge and use of language across the curriculum. A short withdrawal session focusing on a specific curriculum aspect is likely to be useful for the pupil as the practitioner will have the space and time to go into more depth with them than might be possible in a classroom situation.

The best place for EAL learners to do their learning is within their current year group in the mainstream classroom. There are times, however, where it may be appropriate to withdraw learners from the classroom for some specific intervention, e.g. when it is really clear that the whole-class activity can't be made accessible enough for the target learner. Occasionally, older new-to-English learners arrive with very limited education and no literacy in L1. These children have particular needs and will need significant withdrawal intervention to fill in huge gaps in learning, as well as learning the concepts and skills required to read and write at an age-appropriate level.

During withdrawal work, ensure there is a clear language focus and try to keep sessions short – no more than two or three 20-minute sessions per week. Vary the timing in order to avoid missing the same curriculum slots and try to avoid practical lessons or subjects such as languages where EAL learners tend to perform well.

Think carefully about group composition, as it is important for EAL learners to work with peers that can model secure use of language, both orally and within written tasks. Thus, forming groups that only contain beginner EAL learners may not be the most appropriate arrangement.

Finally, identify teachers and TAs that have had specific EAL training; they are likely to be the most successful at withdrawal intervention sessions.

It is important that all tasks meet the cognitive and academic level of the target learners. In addition, learners will benefit from content that has a meaningful context – in other words, work that is directly linked to the curriculum or a sequence of activities that form part of an extended project.

Appropriate activities for withdrawal intervention include the following:

- orientation exercises for new arrivals (Idea 9)
- involvement in an established intervention strategy, e.g. TalkingPartners@Primary (Idea 98)
- pre-teaching of key vocabulary and concepts for upcoming lessons (Idea 42)
- post-teaching to consolidate work from mainstream classes
- games-based activities that focus on oral development for beginner EAL learners
- teaching to address specific gaps in literacy for advanced EAL learners
- extended projects that integrate speaking, listening, reading and writing, such as making talking books, digital storytelling or making videos (see Part 4 in particular).

Taking it further

Collect together a range of resources to make up an intervention toolkit and make it easily accessible for key staff. Useful resources might include: number line/square; historical timeline; puppets; maps; dictionaries; digital recording devices; cheap digital camera; pack of cards and some other common games.

Activate prior knowledge

'EAL learners don't arrive in our classrooms as "blank slates" and neither are they "language disabled", even if they don't know much English.'

Activating prior learning sends 'explicit messages to children that their ideas are of value and that they have an active role to play in their learning' (DfES, Unit 2, 2006, p. 10).

Teaching tip

Activating prior knowledge is not *just* beneficial for EAL learners; draw on the diverse range of languages and cultures of EAL pupils to enrich the learning experience for all pupils. For some British-born monolingual learners, it might be the first time they have met a child from a different ethnicity or heard another language being openly used in the classroom.

Whether UK-born or newly-arrived from abroad, EAL learners have a range of knowledge, skills and experiences influenced by their upbringing and previous schooling. EAL learners might: have missed some schooling or conversely had uninterrupted education; be unused to group work or technology having had a very traditional education abroad; have large gaps in curriculum knowledge but at the same time be way ahead in some subjects such as mathematics and science; only be able to speak and understand their L1 or be highly literate in one or more languages; have lived and/or travelled abroad and know a lot about different countries, cultures and religious traditions; be particularly resilient and adaptable because of circumstance; have developed unusual skills or hobbies that should be recognised and built upon.

Linguistically and culturally responsive teaching takes account of the wider experiences of EAL learners so children can reach their academic potential in the future. Practitioners should have high expectations of all their EAL pupils, recognising their particular strengths and weaknesses and adapting teaching approaches as needed. Effective questioning and peer discussion can identify natural curriculum starting points, along with a KWL grid or concept map (Idea 37) to find out what pupils already know. Use of L1 should be facilitated for shared talk, reading and writing tasks (Idea 26), with culturally familiar references established throughout the curriculum.

Analysing language demands within the curriculum

'At the start of every topic, our Year 5 team map out the different language elements that will need to be explicitly taught to enable all our children to be successful. We recognise this is particularly beneficial for our EAL learners.'

While academic vocabulary is a natural starting point, practitioners will need to look beyond this and consider common grammatical structures and the features of particular text types within different subject disciplines.

EAL learners experience the double challenge of having to learn curriculum content alongside the academic language associated with different subjects and activities. It is therefore essential that practitioners consider the specific language demands of any particular curriculum area and plan their lessons accordingly.

Observing peers in their teaching and watching pre-recorded sessions will enable practitioners to unravel the particular language needed for EAL learners to access key tasks as well as demonstrate full achievement. In this way, specific language demands can be identified and written into curriculum plans.

The language embedded within any subject or activity inherently involves the use of specialist vocabulary and frequently-used phrases as well as the more specific functions and features of both oral and written language. Some EAL learners have already mastered many of these subject-specific language conventions in their L1, while others may have significant gaps. But planning to tackle the language demands of the curriculum will benefit not only EAL learners but also their monolingual peers, as everyone needs to learn academic language that goes beyond everyday situations.

Teaching tip

The following headings (adapted from Gibbons, 1991) could be used in a planning frame for analysing language demands within a topic: Curriculum objectives (desired outcomes); Key activities (what will be done by learners); Language functions (techniques required in use of language); Language features (tone, style, voice, figurative language, grammar); Language structures (examples of sentence starters, linking words, etc.); and Academic vocabulary (context-related words).

Planning using Cummins' framework

'I often advise teachers to use the Cummins framework when planning modules of work for classes with EAL learners.'

The Cummins framework helps teachers to structure lessons that focus on cognitively-challenging, curriculum-related tasks with enough support and scaffolding.

Taking it further

To find out more about Cummins' framework visit: https://ealresources. bell-foundation.org.uk/ eal-specialists/research-1970s-onwards-jim-cummins

Jim Cummins, a Canadian educationalist, developed the Cummins matrix, also called the Cummins framework. This is a grid with two axes; the vertical axis is concerned with cognitive challenge and the horizontal axis is concerned with the context for language learning. Context describes the place for learning as well as the other people and supports involved. This produces four quadrants, A–D, where A is cognitively undemanding and context reduced; B is cognitively undemanding and context embedded; C is cognitively demanding and context embedded; and D is cognitively demanding and context reduced.

EAL pupils who are new to English may be supported by tasks that are in quadrant B in the early stages, e.g. talking to friends while playing a game or matching words and pictures in a geography topic. But spending too long on low-level tasks will not lead to rapid progress in either language or subject content learning. Tasks falling in quadrant C, which are both cognitively challenging and context embedded are going to be the most productive long term. Quadrant C tasks could include:

- A practical science lesson where the EAL learner can hear adults and pupils talking about an experiment while observing it in progress. They can see what it is they need to describe. When they hear new phrases like 'the water is giving off steam' or 'the magnet attracts the paper clip', they have a context they can relate it to.

- A set of instructions to sequence after watching a demonstration of a technique, such as measuring an angle using a protractor or following a recipe.
- Reading a paragraph and extracting keywords to label a diagram or complete a graphic organiser (Idea 39).

The intention is that working within quadrant C provides a rich context for EAL learners in all lessons, so teachers can plan for high cognitive challenge. Context can be provided through the use of visuals, real artefacts and experiences, graphic organisers or practical activities.

Work in quadrant A is not recommended as it contains low-level, meaningless activities, such as copying notes from the board or repeating language drills. Work in quadrant D is independent learning, such as writing an essay or an exam question, with little or no contextual support at all; this will be much harder for beginner EAL learners.

Bonus idea ★

Here is a training idea for teaching staff. Pick out some of the A-D quadrant activity examples mentioned (left) and/or develop your own. Type them up on to little cards. Provide staff with a blank diagram and ask staff to match the activity card to the appropriate A-D quadrant.

Bloom's taxonomy

'Just because my English beginners cannot express as much as their peers in terms of speaking and writing doesn't mean that they are cognitively disabled.'

It is important to provide cognitively demanding tasks for learners, whatever their current English proficiency. Bloom's revised taxonomy provides a practical framework for planning appropriately challenging work, with activities higher up the framework requiring more differentiation than those lower down.

Try reviewing Bloom's revised taxonomy (Krathwohl, 2002) on a regular basis to ensure activities challenge learners to use their higher-order thinking skills, such as creating and evaluating, alongside lower-level processes such as the simple process of remembering. With appropriate support, most EAL learners can reach every level on the framework.

At times, you will want to plan relatively simple tasks that give learners an immediate sense of achievement, e.g. naming objects on flashcards, labelling diagrams, sequencing story visuals and conducting dictionary races. However, you also need to design much more sophisticated activities, such as asking learners to analyse information from a range of sources and argue a case or talk/write persuasively in favour of a particular position. As you work your way up the framework, learners will require increased support to access content, participate orally and create 'written outcomes'. An example from the top-level might be when learners are asked to evaluate a scientific method. Bloom's approaches include questioning that promotes higher-order thinking skills, encouraging pupil use of L1 for oral and written outputs and adjusting expectations in terms of outcome.

Bonus idea ★

Purchase, or create for yourself, a set of Bloom's taxonomy thinking dice. This resource comprises a set of six differently coloured dice representing the six levels on Bloom's taxonomy framework. The six faces on each dice represent trigger questions framed at the appropriate level, e.g. the bottom level might be *'What is . . . '* whereas at the top level it might be *'How many ways can you . . . '*. The dice can be used in lots of ways to improve thinking and questioning skills.

Have flexible curriculum outcomes

'EAL learners are entitled to access the same curriculum as their peers but may need to demonstrate learning differently.'

Practitioners must look beyond the predominately mono-modal output that is written English. Offering different ways for pupils to show their understanding will allow practitioners to track progress more effectively.

How are learners expected to demonstrate progress and attainment within any particular curriculum area? This is an important question because every EAL learner is at a different stage in the acquisition of English. In particular, those newer to English will struggle to demonstrate the full extent of their learning through a predominantly written outcome. For beginner EAL learners:

- Look for feedback through facial expression, mime and gesture.
- Facilitate use of mini-whiteboards, encouraging learners to produce regular visual feedback about their learning through ticks, smiley faces, etc.
- Employ a traffic light system for pupil feedback, with green demonstrating full understanding, amber indicating the pupil is unsure and red indicating confusion.
- Where possible, use bilingual interpreters to help facilitate oral feedback.
- Encourage learners to note-take, annotate work and produce audio/writing in L1, with translation into English later if needed.
- Understanding can be conveyed through drawings/pictures and completion of graphic organisers (Idea 39), e.g. tables, charts, diagrams and mind maps (Idea 37).
- Enable learners to show learning through digital media such as digital photographs, audio recordings and short video clips.

Teaching tip

Evidencing pupil progress can be problematic with beginner EAL learners because they are usually unable to match the range and regularity of expected output as their peers. For this reason, it is a good idea to create an ongoing digital portfolio of pupils' work across the curriculum. *Book Creator* (available on PC, Android and iOS) is a perfect tool as it enables a learner to incorporate text, drawings, photographs, audio and video recordings into ever-expanding digital books. As a result, beginner EAL learners will have a variety of ways to interact with the curriculum, use their L1 as a tool for learning and show their developing use of English in different contexts over time.

Target setting

'Rates of progress for EAL learners need to exceed those for monolingual peers so that they can close the gap and achieve age-related expectations.'

School assessment managers should use ambitious progress models for EAL learners who start from a low baseline but make rapid progress as their English fluency develops.

Teaching tip

When using assessment manager tools to set targets, you may need to override the numerical targets produced when there is no Foundation Stage Profile (FSP) or KS1 baseline, as the algorithms will default to an average expectation, whereas EAL learners usually make faster-than-average progress at early stages of learning English. It is important to consider all the external variables and get a reliable baseline assessment using specialist EAL frameworks (Idea 14). The Fischer Family Trust (FFT) *Student Explorer* is a very good tool for this process.

All EAL learners should be working towards both language and curricular targets, whether they are new-to-English, beginners or more advanced learners. It is important to ensure that targets are appropriate, achievable and challenging and are reviewed on a regular basis. It is also good practice to involve learners in the development and review of their own targets.

Appropriate targets need to match the stage of language development of the learner. Some targets may operate globally across the curriculum, while others need to be designed within a more subject-specific context. Compare the following targets: 'Begin to use paragraphs' and 'Begin to demarcate science investigation reports using topic headings'. Subject-specific targets work best when they support a wider global target; this helps to ensure that all practitioners take responsibility for 'language teaching' rather than just leaving it to the English department or EAL key worker.

It is good practice to create individual language plans (ILPs) for EAL learners at different levels of proficiency in order to establish a whole-school focus on specific aspects of speaking, listening, reading and writing *across* the curriculum.

Curriculum access

Part 3

Linguistic and cultural barriers within the curriculum

'It is easy to make erroneous assumptions about the cultural understandings that children have about their world, whether UK-born or not.'

Each subject area is infused with linguistic and cultural aspects that place EAL learners at a disadvantage compared to their non-EAL peers. This is particularly true of new arrivals or even UK-born children whose parents were educated abroad.

Teaching tip

Even though formal written questions, especially those in exams, are often unsupported visually, it is not helpful to deprive EAL learners of context when *practising* how to approach these types of questions. Therefore, do provide visual elements and oral explanations to ensure that context is clear.

Often as practitioners, 'we don't know what we don't know' when it comes to the linguistic and cultural understandings of our pupils. What words can they understand? What experiences have they had/not had? Each pupil is different and it can be difficult to predict what children do or don't know. This is compounded by the potential range of contexts within which the curriculum is embedded and the way in which language is used in worksheets, textbooks, examination questions and even on the internet.

To illustrate this complexity, consider this mathematical problem (paraphrased from a real example):

> *At yesterday's match 650 people watched Arsenal play on the big screen. Half of these fans bought a programme at £2.50 each. How many fans paid out?*
> *How much money was spent on programmes altogether?*

Ironically, the attempt to make this question accessible for most children makes it very hard for EAL learners, particularly those newer to English. Here are a few linguistic and socio-cultural observations about this question:

- The whole question is expressed very colloquially.

- There is no visual information to provide context.
- This context is about football (although the sport is not mentioned explicitly) – something that the pupil may or may not understand from the name of the football club.
- There are a variety of homographs – 'match', 'fan' and 'programme'.
- The word 'fans' (*half of these fans*) relates to the word 'people' (*650 people*) – critical for understanding what is being asked.
- Pupils need to know that a programme is a booklet you buy at a football match (and that it is not referring to a programme that you watch on TV).
- The use of 'paid out', like many phrasal verbs, can be hard for EAL learners.
- There are two parts to the question and it can be confusing to know what information is required to solve each part.
- The pupil needs to know that the word 'altogether' implies that multiplication (or addition) is required.

> **Bonus idea** ★
>
> Try to develop a standardised text marking scheme to highlight significant elements that comprise a question or problem, e.g. use different coloured highlighters to mark key information, process words (explain, insert, label, tick, complete, use, join, round, measure, etc.) and homographs that might cause confusion.

L1 as a tool for learning across the school

'You wouldn't stop a child thinking in their first language, so why stop them talking, reading and writing if it helps them with their learning?'

Children at an early stage of learning English can benefit enormously from using their first language skills to support their learning. Knowing when to positively encourage this and when to draw pupils away from this strategy requires careful mediation by professionals.

Teaching tip

Use your bilingual learners as a resource within the classroom. They can enrich the lives of other children in the class by conversing in other languages, writing in different scripts and offering interesting verbal and mathematical insights.

Bonus idea ★

Use your pupils (with support from parents and other bilingual adults) to help develop the print environment across the school with multilingual materials. This might include: a multilingual welcome poster in the school office; dual-language signage around the school; dual-language keywords in classrooms; translated menus in the dinner hall; or samples of L1 writings on classroom/corridor walls.

As already discussed (Idea 17), it helps to group same-language learners together so they can collaborate in a preferred language during oral and written tasks. Supply bilingual dictionaries and digital translation tools (Ideas 29 and 30) so that bilingual learners can transfer knowledge from L1 to L2. Encourage more advanced learners to annotate texts in L1 during reading tasks. This will link academic and linguistic knowledge acquired in other situations and help with internalising new language. Provide EAL learners with vocabulary/phrase notebooks to build up personal bilingual language lists.

Learners can also use L1 in writing tasks. Allow beginner EAL learners to note-take and draft writing in a more familiar language. This will enable them to order their thoughts and write more freely, making and correcting mistakes as they progress. There is sound educational thinking in this approach, as they will be able to partake in cognitively demanding work where they will be developing subject knowledge alongside their peers. At a later time, you may be able to get the writing translated. Moreover, more advanced EAL learners will begin to make partial translations for themselves, e.g. by writing a sentence or so in English after they have done the L1 drafting.

Practise message abundancy

'Oversimplification of the curriculum is one of the least successful strategies a practitioner can employ for their EAL learners.'

Rather than making work easier, EAL pupils require explicit teaching that communicates the main message of the lesson in several different ways. Pauline Gibbons (2008), who coined the phrase 'message abundancy', talks about amplifying the message rather than simplifying it.

Instead of simplifying tasks for EAL learners, use 'message abundancy' techniques – teaching sequences that present the key messages in a variety of ways. This offers several opportunities for learners to pick up and absorb new language and concepts.

In certain situations, message abundancy happens naturally, e.g. when giving oral explanations, practitioners tend to make the same point several times using mime, gesture and plenty of visual clues. During question-and-answer sessions, learners also appreciate how practitioners seamlessly recast their language, correcting mistakes naturally by replacing colloquial terminology with more academic forms, e.g. in a science discussion, recasting a sentence using the word 'mass' when the learner had erroneously used the word 'weight'. EAL learners benefit from having several opportunities to access the same curriculum content. A sequence might include the following: watching a short video clip, followed by text marking of written material and finally having a paired discussion that draws out the main points.

Taking it further

To find out more about 'message abundancy', see: Gibbons, P. (2008). 'Challenging Pedagogies: More than just good practice?'. *NALDIC Quarterly*, 6(2), 4–14.

Teaching tip

Reading tasks can be supported by DARTs (Idea 67). In preparation for writing tasks, it can be useful to encourage learners to partially process information using graphic organisers (Idea 39). Additionally, talk-for-writing approaches enable learners to revisit more formal use of language and concepts – useful activities include oral presentations, opinion line debates (Idea 59) and hot-seating (Idea 54). Of course, modelling expected outcomes is also crucial for EAL learners.

Comprehensible input

'The best situation for learning a second language occurs when teachers provide "comprehensible input" in low-anxiety situations, containing messages that students really want to hear.'

Stephen Krashen (1982) introduced some key principles of second language learning, and the implications of his work are far-reaching for EAL teaching.

Taking it further

After a few months, start drawing attention to the *way* we say or write things. Highlight verb forms and comparative language, how we modify nouns, etc.

Teaching tip

Top tips for ensuring a 'comprehensible input' include monitoring your own language by giving clear instructions and avoiding colloquial/metaphorical phrases; not forcing new-to-English pupils to speak before they are ready; rephrasing oral contributions at word and sentence level rather making explicit reference to incorrect grammar; and ensuring that the learner feels comfortable in your class with sympathetic peer (or adult) support.

The first principle is that learners acquire a second language by understanding messages. They will produce their own language when they are ready; it is the teacher's role to provide real communicative and 'comprehensible input', and not force the learner to speak or force correct production and pronunciation through exercises or drills.

Krashen highlights the difference between acquisition and learning. In the initial stages of learning, the learner focuses on listening, understanding and making meaning. After this period of 'acquisition', a learner starts to self-correct or 'monitor' the language they produce, taking notice of grammar rules. For this 'monitoring' to work, more advanced EAL learners need teachers to focus on the structure and forms of the new language.

Another of Krashen's principles is the 'affective filter' which explains how the learner is affected by external variables such as motivation, self-confidence and anxiety. Krashen claims that learners with high motivation, a good self-image, and a low level of anxiety are better equipped for success in second language acquisition. Schools need to provide a safe settled environment from the start, then some general support for curriculum access. But there is also a continued need for specialist language teaching, years after learners have achieved oral fluency, to consolidate their learning.

Bilingual dictionaries

'I know that word in my own language. Using the dictionary gives me confidence in my work.'

When used properly, bilingual dictionaries help pupils transfer knowledge between languages. However, pupils need to learn how to maximise use of such materials or else they may prove to be an unhelpful distraction or even confuse the learner.

Build up a comprehensive range of bilingual dictionaries in the library ready to be loaned to EAL learners when required. Parents of older bilingual children can purchase small, portable dictionaries for their children to take to school every day. Print-only bilingual dictionaries will only be useful when learners have well-developed literacy in L1. You may find that learners who are insecure in sequencing the letters of the English alphabet take too long to find the right word in the dictionary. For this reason, they may be better off with visual dictionaries that tend to organise words thematically.

Just because older bilingual learners have the ability to translate between languages does not mean they know how to make the best use of a dictionary. Ensure learners don't just translate the first matching word they find in the dictionary. They should be aware that some words have homographs and they need to consider each meaning to be sure they have the correct word before translation. They will also benefit from knowing how to use phonetic spelling to pronounce words.

During writing tasks, some learners construct texts in their head using their L1, making a translation into English before committing the words to paper. Encourage them to look up translations of words that they know in L1 to help develop a more varied English vocabulary.

> **Teaching tip**
>
> A useful activity involves bilingual pupils making their own 'page(s)' for a bilingual visual dictionary. Either choose the word(s) for them or let them choose for themselves. They need to illustrate each page with a suitable graphic and add definitions for each word in both languages.

> **Bonus idea** ★
>
> It is possible to source bilingual dictionaries that provide audio support through Mantra Lingua's TalkingPEN technology (Idea 57). The *My Bilingual Talking Dictionary* series is organised thematically and is available in at least 36 languages. With a TalkingPEN, a child can touch each word and hear it pronounced in L1 so that they can make connections between literacy in their own language and English.

Making the most of translation tools

'Having access to a translation tool can be a real life-saver when a bilingual adult is unavailable.'

Routine access to translation tools, both in and out of the classroom, is an essential element of any practitioner's armoury. Understanding the specific strengths and weaknesses of all the available technologies will minimise the chances of making embarrassing mistakes.

Practitioners can make effective use of translation tools for resource preparation prior to a lesson. However, they will need to ensure they know which language is the pupil's strongest language (as the child may know several) and, where needed, that the pupil is literate enough to read anything printed/written in that L1.

Teachers could prepare simple, concise lesson aims that will give unambiguous, meaningful translations. They can also prepare dual-language keyword lists, bearing in mind that some words have a number of homographs. Web-based translation tools are improving all the time, with the possibility of moving far beyond simple word-for-word translation. A tool like *Google Translate* uses context to pull translation from known quality equivalents around the internet. Consequently, some languages are more accurate than others due to the quantity of texts available in different languages.

New-to-English learners should have access to a range of different technologies during lessons to clarify everyday language as well as more academic terminology. This could be through online translation tools, browser plug-ins

Bonus idea ★

You can use an app like *Google Translate* and the camera on your tablet/phone to 'scan' printed text in one language and translate it into a range of other languages. If you install the various different language packs, you can even use the technology in situations where there is no internet connection.

or portable devices and associated apps. Encourage older same-language speakers to talk about translation and make comparisons between languages; this will help learners to notice patterns that make sense to them and allow them to think about structure and purpose in their use of language.

Connected portable devices such as tablets and phones have particular resonance for the classroom. Apps can provide instant word- and sentence-level translations of digital text, which is so much quicker than using a traditional paper-based bilingual dictionary. Moreover, modern apps now enable two-way bilingual conversations. Using an app such as *SayHi,* the in-built microphone can 'listen' for speech, render that on-screen, translate the text and output this in a synthesised voice. This avoids the need to type text before translation and enables children who are not fully literate in L1 to benefit as well.

Quizzing and voting tools

'I don't like to put my hand up in class. I don't want to look stupid.'

A class vote is one way that EAL learners can participate on an equal footing with non-EAL peers.

A quick quiz/vote provides a simple AfL opportunity for practitioners. It enables children to participate in quizzes and class discussions/debates without the need for a significant oral contribution. Physically, they are easy enough to set up using laminated cards. Agree/disagree votes could use thumbs-up/thumbs-down or ticks/crosses; multiple-choice quizzes and opinion lines (Idea 59) could use cards labelled with numbers or letters.

Quizzing/voting apps enable learners to give opinions or answer questions more anonymously, so it is not apparent to peers what 'answer' has been provided. However, with many quizzing/voting tools, it is also possible to set up the app so that the practitioner knows how each pupil has responded.

Digital quizzing/voting tools work in different ways – some require access to a computer or mobile device, while others use the camera on a portable device and voting cards, each of which contains a unique code.

Some free digital tools include *Answer Garden* (https://answergarden.ch), a website and app that collates typed responses visually in a word cluster for the whole class to view on the IWB; *Plickers* (www.plickers.com), an app that uses the camera on a mobile device to record a pupil's response made by holding up a card containing a unique code; and *Socrative* (www.socrative.com), a website and apps with similar functionality to *Plickers* but with a wireless connection needed.

Interactive whiteboards (IWBs), data projectors and visualisers

'Once my pupils are focused towards the whiteboard I can scan their faces. It gives me immediate feedback on whether they are comprehending my input or not.'

Projecting onto a whiteboard is a great way to help EAL learners focus on a specific item of interest. You can highlight specific content, enlarge resources, deliver multimedia content and model practical or literacy-based learning.

IWBs provide useful functionality for teaching and learning, with the touch-sensitive surface of an IWB offering all learners an additional method of interacting with the curriculum with no speaking or writing involved, e.g. through drawing, highlighting and drag-and-drop interactions. Visualisers also add another dimension to teaching, allowing you to make meaning more explicit for EAL learners. They are useful for enlarging or examining small organisms or artefacts and perfect for showing a top-down view of how to do something, e.g. modelling cursive script, modelling the correct use of a calculator or protractor, or demonstrating how to measure distance on a map using a piece of string. It is also possible to perform shared reading, with the advantage of being able to show the visuals alongside the text.

Visualisers provide an immediate way to show the whole class a piece of work in progress, e.g. group planning in the form of a storyboard, or a first draft of a piece of writing. This helps to model expectations for learners and encourage peer review. You can also get wireless versions of visualisers, so that you can walk around the room and project work instantly onto the whiteboard with minimum interruption to the class.

Bonus idea ★

It's possible to use a tablet as a visualiser using software like *iVisualiser*, available from Apple's App Store. This has two modes of operation. You can take a picture with the camera or import an image from the camera roll and then use the in-built tools to annotate over the top of the still image. The app also allows you to annotate over the top of a live video feed from the tablet's camera. It's possible to take a screen shot of whatever annotations have been made in either mode of operation.

Maximising use of mobile devices – tablets and phones

'I am forever using my phone to communicate simple ideas to my pupils using their language.'

Mobile devices have tremendous potential for supporting EAL learners because they promote multimodal learning through clearly rendered text, high-quality audio-visual elements and kinaesthetic, gesture-based interactivity.

While mobile technologies can be very personal learning devices, their portability also makes them effective for collaborative learning (Idea 53), as the devices can easily be shared within a group learning situation, particularly tablets with larger screens. The touch-sensitive, gesture-based mode of operation can also support learners who may be unfamiliar with the use of complicated operating systems, keyboards and mice. Translation apps (Idea 30) offer practitioners the opportunity to convey simple ideas and have short conversations with their pupils.

Mobile devices all feature eBook reading technology, and finding and managing books and articles (in any language) is easy through the use of apps like *iBooks* and *Kindle*. Many books provide a fully immersive experience through text, animated images and the ability to listen to professionally recorded narration. Digital texts can also be read aloud using the in-built text-to-speech synthesis offered by the mobile device. Users have access to context-sensitive dictionaries and potentially translation capability as well. These tools are perfect for supporting emergent readers.

Mobile devices can be used to support learning across the curriculum, facilitating acquisition of target language in context and offering

Bonus idea ★

Some EAL learners might benefit from playing around with the various voice assistants incorporated into modern technology e.g. *Google Assistant*, *Siri*, *Cortana* or *Alexa*. These technologies listen out for natural questions and are a quick way to search for answers on mobile devices. Not only do they short-cut the need to type accurately but learners will be able to practise their speech and improve their ability to ask natural questions by judging whether or not the system registers correctly and provides sensible answers.

beginner EAL learners in particular different ways of demonstrating understanding. The camera allows children to integrate images and video into creative curriculum-based projects such as digital storytelling (Idea 45), producing graphic texts (Idea 72), delivering oral presentations via talking avatars (Idea 58), making talking books (Idea 44) or making videos (Idea 46).

Supportive word processors (Idea 78) enable pupils to easily integrate text (in any language), images/video and sound together in documents as well as providing error-checking tools. Text-to-speech (Idea 68) can read back what has been written and speech-to-text can enable a pupil to enter text quickly via voice rather than on-screen typing.

In order to maximise use of mobile devices ensure that:

- You find a suitable way to connect the device to data projector-adapters, software (e.g. AirServer®) or hardware.
- The in-built text-to-speech option is enabled within the device's settings.
- Children understand how to enter text via speech-to-text within different apps.
- Soft keyboards are set up for the different L1s used by literate EAL learners in the school.
- Supportive word processors are installed, e.g. *Book Creator* and *Clicker Docs.*
- Dictionary tools like *Dictionary.com* are installed.
- Creative apps for storytelling, producing comics/graphic texts and talking avatars are also available.
- Two-way translation apps like *SayHi* are readily accessible.

Taking it further

Check out some suitable apps for primary age EAL learners: http:// documents.hants. gov.uk/education/ EMTASPrimaryPhaseApp Wheel.docx.

Use of images

'At the beginning, I got bored because I didn't know the words. The pictures gave me a clue to what was going on.'

Access to good-quality images, whether printed or digital, is essential for working with EAL learners. There really is truth in the old adage that a picture is worth a thousand words; a carefully chosen image will make ideas and concepts much more explicit.

It is worth building up a good selection of images to support topics or subjects across the curriculum. Try developing cognitively demanding tasks for new-to-English learners that are non-verbal and kinaesthetic in nature, such as those that require manipulation of printed or digital images. Encourage learners to:

- Sort photographs based on particular criteria, such as a historical time period.
- Use collage as a framework for comparing and contrasting ideas such as settings, characters or themes within or between familiar stories.
- Match images together, e.g. photographs of art from the same artist, style or artistic movement.
- Rank images on set criteria such as mathematical scale.
- Develop a visual narrative from a set of images to explain a sequence of events, e.g. a physical, chemical or biological process, the causes of a historical incident or an environmental disaster.
- Choose historical visual sources to support a particular point of view.
- Interpret details in one image by overlaying with another, such as when matching a map to a satellite photograph.
- Predict details in obscured parts of an image, e.g. continue a trend in a graph or draw in the missing organisms in a food web.

Images are also excellent for developing oracy and literacy across the curriculum. Projecting images onto the whiteboard (Idea 43) at the start of a lesson helps to contextualise work coming up later or to recap content from a previous lesson. Get learners to discuss a mystery object, find the link between a rolling set of images or spot the odd one out. Show a close-up of an image and ask the class to theorise about its identity – this is an excellent way to model the use of modal verbs. Images also help support show-and-tell activities and presentations, as well as forming the focus for class debates (Idea 59).

Get learners to talk in depth about one or more images; this encourages the use of more formal talk that helps to bridge the gap between thinking, talking and writing. Some learners have difficulty with annotating their own artwork; reviewing each other's work helps reinforce technical language and model language structures that they will need to use in their writing. Talking about historical or geographical visual sources will help learners pick out relevant language for extended writing activities.

Annotating images, digitally or in print also helps develop media literacy. Ask learners to write a caption for what is happening in a photograph or design a snappy slogan for a product. Ask them to annotate different parts of an image, e.g. an X-ray or ultrasound, a painting of the crucifixion, an image of war, a photograph of a disaster zone or a Heath Robinson drawing. Again, short annotations encourage the use of a more formal, academic style of writing, particularly for description and explanation. You can also stimulate creative writing by getting learners to talk and write about a series of connected book illustrations without the text.

> **Bonus idea** ★
>
> Try getting pupils to annotate an image such as an advertisement, poster or photograph using chunks of text that can then be used to inform a wider piece of writing. Practising vocabulary and short phrases in a written format is an effective bridge to more extensive writing.

Use of audio

'I can get more meaning if the words are read aloud to me.'

As they progress through the early stages of acquiring English, many EAL learners hear and understand better than they read and write. Presenting a key text or other information orally is a simple way to open up access to the curriculum.

Taking it further

Check out the Audio Network, which has a large curated set of free-to-use audio files for educational purposes (www.nen.gov.uk/learning-resources/audio-network).

Providing learners with oral access to key texts makes meaning more explicit for EAL learners. Oral versions of books and poems can often be found on CDs, and audiobooks can be listened to on many eBook readers. Digital texts can be read aloud from a computer/mobile device via text-to-speech technology (Ideas 33 and 68) in real-time.

Find audio files or podcasts that demonstrate particular aspects of language use across the curriculum. You could play famous speeches to demonstrate use of formal, standard English. Radio plays or shows can model more informal talk and highlight the differences in regional accents. A quick search on the internet can reveal lots of podcasts for reinforcing curricular learning. There are also podcasts that focus more on the conversational language required for different everyday contexts.

Songs can be useful for consolidating what learners already know; they lend themselves naturally to listening tasks – learners can listen to songs like 'Dem Bones' or 'The Elements', identifying key scientific vocabulary. Certain songs are perfect for demonstrating particular grammatical features, and lyrics can be used for active listening and associated reading activities such as text marking and reconstruction exercises. Don't forget how powerful music is for conveying meaning. A suitable sample of music could be useful for reinforcing metre and mood in a particular poem.

Use of video

'My mum showed me a video about Henry VIII on the internet. It helped me with my project work.'

Judicial use of video can reinforce hard-to-explain topics within any subject area. While video clips can obviously support in-class learning, there is also a place for a more blended approach with children accessing video content prior to lessons.

Many pupils need substantial help to overcome both linguistic and cultural barriers; for some, topic information can be conveyed more effectively through the combination of sound and image. Short clips will be more effective than extensive sections; beginner EAL learners in particular will find it hard to concentrate on this type of activity for long periods of time. During lessons, prepare one or two questions to focus attention, or provide a simple graphic organiser (Idea 39) in which to record key information.

EAL learners will also appreciate the opportunity to watch films and TV versions of books/plays they are currently studying; this will help reinforce the plot as well as bring characters and settings to life. Films on DVD usually offer the option to show English subtitles, which can be beneficial for some EAL learners. Indeed, it may also be possible to get subtitles in other languages, which may help beginner EAL learners who are literate in L1. Occasionally, try showing video without the sound, as this puts all learners in the same position. Encourage learners to discuss what is happening in the scene, or ask them to consider what just happened or predict what is about to happen.

Teaching tip

EAL learners experience the unique challenge of having to internalise curriculum content at the same time as acquiring new language; this can be very demanding for some pupils. Try to take a more blended approach to learning. Encourage children to view topic-related videos prior to the lesson as this will enable you to spend more time focusing on the language demands of the lesson. Useful websites include TrueTube (www.truetube.co.uk) and BBC Bitesize (www.bbc.co.uk/education).

Mind maps

'Mind maps help my EAL learners to build on prior knowledge and transfer learning from their first language.'

Mind maps are a visual representation of connected information. They give an insight into a learner's current thinking and are an effective way of evaluating their understanding about a particular topic.

Teaching tip

Install mind-mapping software on the school computers as this will speed up the process of producing quality mind maps, e.g. *FreeMind* (www.freemind. sourceforge.net).

A mind map, or concept map, might be used to elicit prior knowledge at the beginning of a topic. Draw one central idea on the whiteboard, and build up a hierarchy of connected words or phrases along different branches of the diagram. Most EAL learners will appreciate time to think and talk through ideas before responding in a whole-class situation. This could also be organised as a small-group activity, with each learner given a different-coloured marker to ensure participation from all learners, and it being the whole group's responsibility to ensure a reasonable spread of colour.

Mind maps can also be developed throughout a topic rather than at the start, and they can be an effective way to summarise learning at the end. In a mind map, learners need to be more organised and consistent about how they link ideas together, keeping each branch of the map to a single colour; this has been shown to assist recall. Suggest that learners annotate with single words or very short phrases, using print rather than writing. Finally, encourage the use of images, symbols or icons, as these can convey ideas more simply than printed words. Encourage learners to use their mind maps as revision aids, or perhaps display them prominently in the classroom. You may also want to keep a colour photocopy of some of the best ones to use as stimulus material for future work.

Key visuals

'Diagrams are much more helpful to my new arrivals than reams of writing.'

Key visuals convey information very succinctly and in a way that often transcends language. Pupils should be given access to suitable key visuals in textbooks and on the web. Equally, they will benefit from manipulating incomplete versions or creating their own to support topic work.

Key visuals are information packages; they aid understanding by showing the relationships between content, concepts and language. They enable learners to move beyond basic 'naming language' into higher-order thinking, including explanation, hypothesis and prediction. In science, for example, food webs and pyramids of numbers conceptually show how organisms are connected with each other and with their environment. Here, the size and position of graphical elements, such as pictures and symbols, imply semantic relationships; together with concise text, they help learners recall both colloquial and academic language.

Introduce a topic by showing a key visual, and keep it in a visible place throughout the work. This is an excellent way to illustrate complex ideas and introduce or reinforce academic language.

Key visuals are self-contained narratives that support the development of explanatory writing. Using a key visual like a 'Heath Robinson' contraption, learners could be required to produce an explanation of how it works. This helps to develop texts that have a logical structure, varied use of academic vocabulary, cause-and-effect language and copious use of time-based cohesive devices.

Teaching tip

Learners can create their own key visuals to help them remember specific information. When studying a book on a historical event, for example, they can produce a story map to illustrate the main plot, settings, characters and so on. The developmental process will help reinforce the sequence of events and main facts, and act as a trigger for information recall at a later date.

Bonus idea ★

Key visuals for certain activities are useful for a wide variety of children and therefore could be made available on a working wall or other public space in the classroom. Use a free tool like PosteRazor (www.posterazor. sourceforge.net) to print large versions so that key visuals are easily viewable from all positions within the classroom.

Graphic organisers

'I don't know where to start. . . there's too much information.'

Use graphic organisers when learners are required to process a lot of information before a formal output such as a presentation or piece of writing.

Graphic organisers take the form of blank templates that act as a holding area for different types of information. As an example:

A Year 5 class has been asked to explore the following question: *Was Henry VIII a hero or a horror?* For this task, the pupils need to collate evidence from a range of sources and use the information to write a discursive text that presents all the arguments. A learner could use a simple table to sort information into two contrasting groups. Alternatively, a Venn diagram might be more appropriate, offering an overlapping area in which to place aspects of Henry's reign that were more neutral or that had both positive and negative impacts. Having part-processed the information, EAL learners will find the language demands of the writing task much easier, because they can simply refer to the table or Venn diagram rather than having to reread the original source material. Staging a task like this really supports EAL learners in more formal oral and written tasks.

Some examples of different types of graphic organisers, arranged by the organisational mechanism they can be used to support, include: sorting (retrieval charts, tree diagrams); sequencing (storyboards, timelines, flow-charts, branching diagrams, cycles); making logical connections (cause and effect diagrams, mind maps (Idea 37)); comparing and contrasting (tables, Venn diagrams); ordering and ranking (ladders, pyramids); and concluding and evaluating (living graphs (Idea 69)).

Finding and using internet-based sources

'I usually select suitable websites for my EAL learners as typically they are unable to discriminate appropriate sources for themselves'

Although some information sources on the internet are designed for younger audiences, most are not. Offering texts to EAL learners that are either not age-appropriate or not easy enough for comprehension is counterproductive.

The internet can be a bewildering place for learners, particularly those still acquiring full academic proficiency in English. Not only are there likely to be numerous sources, but the quality, reliability and level of language will all affect the usefulness of the information. For this reason, it can be a good idea to prepare a limited list of appropriate websites for a particular topic or activity. This will help EAL learners who may otherwise waste a lot of time on irrelevant or inaccessible information.

Utilising effective search techniques will help EAL learners to produce a smaller number of search results with a better match to the initial keywords. Recommended tips and tricks include ensuring that learners limit the number of keywords in searches, don't use high frequency words as part of their searches, check that words are spelled correctly and avoid subject-specific words with double meanings. They should review the number of page results – lower numbers are generally good – and know how to use advanced search techniques. It may be appropriate for older pupils to use proficiency in L1 to search for and access information in a preferred language, while texts beyond the reach of pupils can be opened up through text-to-speech programmes.

Bonus idea ★

Research the most useful child-friendly search engines and information sources, and ensure they are bookmarked on the school's network. A couple of useful websites include: 'Simple English' version of Wikipedia (https://simple.wikipedia.org) and Kid Rex (www.kidrex.org).

The mathematics problem

'Omer has no problem with doing the mathematics, but as soon as he is presented with wordy problems he struggles.'

There is a common assumption that mathematics is a universal language and therefore easier than other subjects for EAL pupils. What practitioners sometimes forget is that UK mathematics has a language all of its own, particularly in the way wordy problems are expressed, which is quite unlike how texts in many other subjects work.

Mathematics provides a good example of the importance of teaching language alongside curriculum content (Idea 42). There is evidence that many EAL learners, as well as their monolingual peers, under-attain because the UK mathematics curriculum has significant language demands. Specific ideas to combat this problem include the following:

- Provide plenty of opportunity to talk about mathematics, e.g. try the Talking Maths programme (Idea 98) or show learners how to break wordy problems down into manageable chunks.
- Focus on academic vocabulary, e.g. the many different terms for each numerical operator.
- Create mathematical calligrams to reinforce learning (see next page).
- Highlight language anomalies – homophones such as 'sine' and 'sign' or homonyms like 'mean', 'power' and 'root', which have several different meanings.

Many learners who have studied mathematics abroad are gifted mathematicians, but have additional cultural hurdles to overcome before they can demonstrate their true ability (Idea 25). They may have learned some areas (e.g. algebra) in significant depth, yet will have missed other topics completely, e.g.

Bonus idea ★

The Collaborative Learning Project has an enormous quantity of mathematical DARTs (Idea 67) that can be downloaded and immediately used or edited for your pupils' specific EAL needs (www.collaborativelearning.org/maths.html).

investigative mathematics. Here are some other issues that may need attention:

- Check whether learners are familiar with the Hindu-Arabic numerals, as they may have used other number systems in their country of origin.
- Clarify how decimal points, multiplication/division signs and other symbols differ in their use from country to country.
- If they are secure, encourage learners to use their own way of solving number problems; note that some methods may be very different to those taught in UK schools.
- Be aware that in some cultures learners rely upon one secure method of solving a problem and may find it difficult to understand the notion of trying alternative methods.

Teaching tip

Try 'reverse engineering' a mathematical problem by starting with a numerical sum and asking pupils to construct a wordy problem around it. You could provide a scenario to set the context and some appropriate keywords that have to be used.

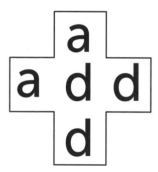

Pre-teaching and reinforcing curriculum-related language

'I like playing games. . . they help me learn new words.'

Pupils need to acquire subject-specific technical vocabulary as well as the process words that are essential to enable pupils to connect and signal ideas in their oral/written outputs.

Teaching tip

Pre-teaching new language should be fun and interactive. Try any of these tools and ideas: language flashcards; vocabulary *Jenga*® (Idea 76); word or sentence dominoes; word searches or crosswords supported by visuals; labelling key visuals; barrier games on a particular topic (Idea 55); bingo – words matched to definitions (Idea 76); paragraph puzzles – where text has been chopped up into words, phrases or whole sentences; 'follow me' activities (Idea 76); sorting words or phrases into graphic organisers (Idea 39); or dictogloss (Idea 75).

Pre-teaching relevant academic language before exposing EAL learners to the main content of a lesson has been shown to be a successful strategy. It helps learners overcome the double challenge of encountering new curriculum content alongside the language demands of the specific task. Focused preparatory language teaching can 'top and tail' lessons or be presented during short-term withdrawal sessions (Idea 18) and out-of-hours clubs.

However pre-teaching is organised, learners should encounter new language within a clear curriculum-related context in order for meaning to be made explicit. In addition, the key language will be best acquired when they can repeatedly see, hear and read new words in order to speak or write them in sentences and apply them in new situations. Academic language should include key vocabulary, common sentence structures and specific cohesive devices. Particular attention should be given to preparing learners for writing within different genres, in a particular register and according to the conventions of specific text types.

Parents and carers are critical partners in helping their children prepare for upcoming work. This might be as simple as talking through a topic with their child, rehearsing a few technical words with vocabulary games provided by the school or visiting some useful websites such as BBC Bitesize (www.bbc.co.uk/education).

Integrated approaches to learning

Part 4

Identity texts

'Children love creating their own stories, particularly when they can relate them to their individual cultural background and use their L1s.'

Identity texts are an effective way of activating prior knowledge as well as providing insights into the linguistic and cultural lives of children that often exist beyond the school gates.

Teaching tip

Set up a free class *Storybird* account (https://storybird.com). This online tool provides a digital playground for children to produce their own stories using thousands of provided images. Using a personalised account, children can work on stories, in any language, from any location. *Storybird* particularly supports home-based learning.

Bonus idea ★

Signing up to *Storybird* also gives access to an app called *Lark*. This online tool gives access to countless images alongside contextual words. Selected words can be dragged onto the chosen image and arranged in any sequence and pattern to create a personalised narrative before sharing and/or printing.

Jim Cummins, a Canadian professor, describes identity texts as artefacts created and owned by children that are literary mirrors, reflecting back a pupil's identity to the viewer/reader. Identity texts can be anything from pure text to talking books (Idea 44), podcasts or even digital stories (Idea 45). EAL learners, particularly those who are relatively new to the school, often feel that their teachers do not know enough about their lives, and this can be compounded for those at the early stages of acquiring English.

Find opportunities for pupils to create identity texts; be aware that some children, particularly those with complex and/or traumatic backgrounds, may be uncomfortable with the idea. Always encourage the use of L1 alongside English. Here are a few ideas for personal topics:

- my life before coming to the UK
- starting at my new school
- a trip to my home country
- a traditional story from my culture
- what my religion means to me
- what it feels like to be bilingual
- being British and from another cultural heritage.

Find out more about Jim Cummins' ideas on identity texts here: www.curriculum.org/secretariat/files/ELLidentityTexts.pdf.

Making talking books

'Paulina loved bringing her story alive with her own voice. She was able to do the narration in Polish and English.'

Creating talking books is a powerful way to seamlessly integrate speaking, listening, reading and writing with the creative arts, alongside cross-curricular use of ICT.

At their simplest, talking books are texts with images and some form of audio component. EAL learners benefit particularly if they can draw upon life experiences or traditional stories from their own cultural background or utilise expertise in their L1 to produce multi-language versions.

Making talking books works best within the mainstream classroom, although it can also be successful in withdrawal intervention sessions (Idea 18). Organise learners into small groups, where EAL learners work alongside peers who can model good use of English. The informal talk generated during group work will be beneficial for beginner EAL learners, and the more formal literacy demands of reading and writing new texts, perhaps with L1 translation, will help more advanced EAL learners.

Inspiration for cross-cultural bilingual stories can be elicited from learners. Several publishers stock a good range of texts, and bilingual stories can also be found on the internet; try the International Children's Digital Library (en.childrenslibrary.org).

You can produce your own multilingual talking books too: paper-based texts can be audio-enabled using TalkingPENs (Idea 57), and computer-based software or apps for mobile devices (such as *Book Creator* for KS2 and *My Story* for EYFS and KS1) allow you to create talking books from digital texts.

Teaching tip

A useful video about making talking books for EAL learners can be found here: www.youtube.com/watch?v=VSgHU34tYmg.

Bonus idea ★

Download 'Developing Reading Skills Through Home Language' for more information on how talking books can help EAL learners (www.rnlcom.com/wp-content/uploads/2015/02/Developing-reading-skills-through-home-languages.pdf).

Digital storytelling – running a project

'Digital storytelling is a perfect way to integrate skills from across the curriculum.'

Digital stories are recorded narratives involving speech, music, text and visual elements, usually bound together in a video-based format.

Teaching tip

A useful video about digital storytelling for EAL learners can be found here: www.youtube.com/ watch?v=4mJ3exsK7FI, while video case studies can be found here: digitalstorytelling.segfl. org.uk.

Taking it further

Provide a slot of time to allow the group to source additional things like clothing, props and digital sounds or music. Narration, music, visuals and text can be bound together using a range of software such as *PowerPoint, Photo Story 3, Puppet Pals HD, Morfo* or *iMovie*.

Projects can span over the course of a week, or try collapsing the timetable into a whole day. Decide on a theme, e.g. traditional tales, stories from other cultures or historical re-enactments

Groups should be well-balanced, with EAL learners working alongside confident English speakers. Prior learning can be activated by encouraging EAL learners to share stories from their own backgrounds and perform retellings in their own language as well as in English.

The first step involves storyboarding. Ask groups to split the narrative into six to eight sections, illustrating a storyboard template with drawings and annotations of what is happening in each scene. The group should decide on a technique for packaging the story, e.g. freeze-frame photographs, video or clay animation.

Narration should be kept to a minimum; the best results are achieved by writing the narration down and ensuring that learners have plenty of time to rehearse. Record audio separately from the visual element, with opportunities to use L1, as this will benefit shy EAL learners who prefer to prepare their oral contribution in private. Encourage them to review their efforts and re-record where necessary.

Organise a showcase at the end, and keep copies for potential assessment purposes.

Digital storytelling – using *iMovie* trailers

'Some of my EAL beginners are just not ready for lots of writing; they can more easily show understanding by making a quick video about the topic.'

Making a film can be quite time-consuming, but mobile devices and apps like *iMovie* can simplify the process – the in-built trailers provide a simple framework for adding images, video and text.

iMovie is a capable video editor, but it's the trailer feature that makes this app such a winner. There are 14 trailers to suit different genres – anything from 'Narrative' to 'Coming of age' to 'Expedition'. The trailers contain replaceable imagery alongside editable text and a non-removable soundtrack. Images and video can be imported straight into the template and short quantities of text can be over-typed. There is no option to include an oral narrative, but it is easy enough to export the video and re-edit it in *iMovie*. Very professional videos can be made within even a one-hour lesson.

There are benefits, too, for collaborative group work with opportunities for pupils to develop colloquial and academic language. Making videos can support learning across the curriculum and enables children to learn different text type conventions without producing lots of writing. Making a video can also act as a bridge to a more formal piece of writing.

Some examples of when to use *iMovie* (with the appropriate trailer) include a personal narrative (narrative, superhero, family); traditional stories (fairy tale, swashbuckler, scary); recount, e.g. a school visit (expedition, coming of age, indie); topic/project report, e.g. a science experiment (retro, adrenaline); instructions/explanations, e.g. a 'How to' guide (family, retro); or a persuasive advert (adrenaline, narrative, expedition).

Teaching tip

Download free *iMovie* trailer templates in a printable format from the Learning in Hand blog (https://learninginhand. com/blog). The templates provide a storyboard framework in which pupils can organise the sequence of their media clips and define the text to overlay each scene.

Bonus idea ★

Another iOS app that provides similar functionality is *Silent Film Studio.* This enables pupils to make a black and white silent film with text panels and an accompanying old-style music score.

Viewing and producing infographics

'Infographics are a powerful way to convey information through comprehensible graphics and succinct use of text.'

Infographics are a popular type of information that can be found everywhere — both in print and on the internet. They are a very versatile educational tool. Primarily, they can be used to provide contextualised information to help learners internalise and repurpose information. However, pupils can also learn a lot from creating their own versions.

Provide pupils with infographics when you need them to access lots of information before a presentation or writing task. You can also give pupils partially-completed infographics and ask them to fill in the blank spaces with content prepared by you or generated by themselves.

Infographics can be sourced from all sorts of different places although it will be necessary to check their provenance. Look out for infographics in magazines and newspapers, and of course they can be found all over the internet with the simplest of searches.

The process of producing their own infographics can help pupils as they revisit and/or discover additional information as well as create new meanings for themselves. The heavily graphical nature of infographics, with minimal use of text, is generally supportive for most EAL learners as it can help them be relatively successful at repurposing topic information without the need to produce large quantities of cohesive text.

Showing EAL learners examples of different types of infographics and sourcing editable templates will be a helpful preparatory step.

Bonus idea ★

Install infographic creators like *Canva* (www.canva.com) or *Easelly* (www.easel. ly) for easy creation of infographics. This type of software offers easily editable templates and additional graphical assets to create professional-looking infographics.

Here are a few ideas for infographic projects:

- Ask pupils to create information about a specific topic, e.g. the events involved in a particular religious festival.
- Invite children to present research findings, e.g. traffic flow dynamics outside the main school gate.
- Task learners with explaining a specific issue, e.g. global warming or animal welfare.
- Encourage learners to create a timeline infographic, e.g. the life of a significant person or a historical event like The Great Fire of London.
- Get pupils to illustrate a geological process using maps, flow diagrams and charts, e.g. an earthquake or a volcanic eruption.
- Challenge learners to make a comparison infographic, e.g. compare and contrast people, places, books or events.
- Inspire pupils to use an infographic to present a weather report or news article.

Playing and making board games

'I find that playing a board game is one of the best ways for me to connect with my new peer buddy.'

Board games tend to be culturally familiar even if the specific game is not. Children can learn colloquial language and even academic language when the game is rooted in the curriculum.

For children who are new to English, board games and similar activities are perfect for generating both colloquial (BICS) and more academic (CALP) language in a familiar context. Board games work on many levels and help to develop important skills, such as logic and strategy; cooperation and turn taking; speaking and listening; repetitive language – vocabulary and short phrases; and academic language (when curriculum-based).

For small-group withdrawal intervention sessions:

1. Choose any well-known traditional multiplayer board game with simple rules. This is an excellent opportunity for EAL learners to teach their peers a game that comes from their own cultural background.
2. Select a target group of beginner EAL learners and one or more articulate English speakers.
3. Support with an additional adult.
4. Provide game-playing oral prompt sheets where necessary (Idea 52).

Literacy through digital games

'I like to use digital games to focus on specific text types — for example, recount, explanation or persuasion.'

The best digital games are those that have been professionally designed, with strong narratives and a truly immersive multimedia experience. Try not to use those designed to teach English as they tend to be no more than thinly disguised tests.

Digital games are usually very familiar to pupils, even those newly arrived from abroad. A suitable age-appropriate game can be used to stimulate interest and provide a focus for improving speaking, listening, reading and writing within different genres and text types.

Choose games that have a strong narrative, immersive sounds, music and graphics, authentic texts, cryptic puzzles and, where possible, clear links to the curriculum. It is not desirable or necessary to play the whole game fully. Instead, play significant parts such as the introduction and ending. Rather than getting the children to play the game individually or in small groups, it can be more successful when the game is played as a whole class.

Here are a few ideas for using digital games:

- Facilitate speaking and listening by obtaining a game walkthrough and asking one child to give instructions to another about how to play a specific part of the game.
- Focus on descriptive writing by immersing the pupils in unusual or particularly beautiful game settings.
- Practise recount by asking pupils to write a game section walkthrough.
- Teach an explanation style by getting pupils to explain how to solve a puzzle in the game.

Taking it further

Check out a British Council research project that investigated how immersive games can be used to develop writing for more advanced EAL learners. The project contains a video case study, research report and associated resources and can be found here: https://ealresources. bell-foundation.org.uk/ eal-specialists/eal-and-immersive-games.

Bonus idea ★

Find professionally produced game advertisements via the internet and use them as a stimulus to a digital gaming unit. Analyse game advertisements for bias and ask pupils to spot all the persuasive devices that have been used. Children could even create their own advertisements through digital media.

Encouraging speaking and listening

Part 5

Understand the difference between BICS and CALP

'Sameena has only been here for six months, and she is already speaking fluently!'

New-to-English learners acquire basic spoken language quickly compared with the language of learning, which takes much longer.

Taking it further

Model to advanced EAL learners how we use 'analytical verbs' rather than spoken verbs in our writing, e.g. rather than using the common everyday word 'make', be specific with verbs like 'manufacture', 'produce' or 'construct'. These in turn can be transformed into abstract nouns to talk about the processes themselves, e.g. 'manufacturing', 'production' and 'construction'.

Professor Jim Cummins highlights the difference and continuum between Basic Interpersonal Communication Skill (BICS), the speech of everyday life, and Cognitive Academic Language Proficiency (CALP), the language that we use in school learning.

EAL learners acquire BICS through speaking and listening in everyday situations, supported by context – their surroundings, visuals, objects, gestures, etc. It generally takes one or two years to acquire BICS and be confident speakers of English in most situations. In contrast, CALP is learnt rather than acquired. It is linked to the thoughts, concepts and processes taught within school and learning. CALP is much more abstract and likely to be 'context reduced', found mainly in written texts and with fewer visual supports.

Research suggests that CALP can often take seven to ten years to develop, especially when the learners do not have secure literacy in their L1. Many EAL learners' progress stalls after three or four years and this is when they need additional teaching to support the development of CALP across the curriculum. Focus on developing exploratory talk, supporting inference while reading, introducing academic words to replace everyday vocabulary (*give out = distribute, emit, disseminate, etc.) and* modelling writing for every new task.

Effective questioning techniques

'My beginners rarely, if ever, answer questions in a whole-class discussion'.

A perennial worry for many practitioners is the lack of interaction by EAL learners during teacher-led discussions, especially in whole-class situations. This can be true for both beginner and advanced learners. While recognising that it is important to respect an initial silent phase for those new to English, before long such learners should be taking part along with their peers.

Here are some useful tips to encourage all learners to participate in oral discussions.

- Establish a culture that encourages all learners to take risks without the worry of being wrong.
- Employ the use of mini-whiteboards and visual feedback systems (Idea 31); these enable reticent talkers to participate visually at first, encouraging more oral contribution in the future.
- Initiate a 'no hands up' rule, allowing you to control who attempts to answer questions.
- Use more open-ended questions that require greater detail or that have a number of possible answers; these questions give learners more opportunity to show what they do and don't know.
- Avoid using idiomatic language, which is very hard for most EAL learners to understand.
- Give learners plenty of thinking time prior to asking for a response.
- Encourage learners to discuss the question in pairs or groups of three, providing an opportunity to rehearse answers. Be sure to group EAL learners appropriately (Idea 17).
- Where individuals or groups need to report back in turn, allow beginners to take their turn later in the sequence so that they can hear answers being modelled by their peers.

Teaching tip

Avoid closed questions that require yes/no or single-word answers, except for complete beginners who you feel sure will benefit from getting the answer correct in front of their peers.

Taking it further

Take a look at Marion Blank's four levels of questions in order to find out how to make questioning more effective and formalised throughout the whole school. There are many free resources on the internet that have been adapted from Blank's ideas.

Talk prompts

'Sometimes EAL learners need help with knowing how to begin a question or answer or even to say something more academic such as giving their opinion about a curriculum-related topic.'

It is well established that writing frames can help emergent writers. Talk prompts work in a similar way in that they give pupils confidence by providing typical starter phrases and connecting statements to encourage learners to participate in a range of different oral contexts.

Those learners who are emerging from a silent phase or who are reticent speakers will benefit from scaffolding to support talk. In order to encourage learners to participate in class discussions, group work and presentations, oral prompts should be available in an easily accessible format. Some learners will be able to read and use simple written forms, whereas others may require digitally recorded versions.

At their simplest, talk prompts are open-ended sentence starters and commonly used phrases designed to prompt the colloquial language needed for collaborative activities, e.g. when playing a board game: *It's your/my turn/go; Roll the dice; Move. . . spaces; Miss your turn/ go; Pick up a card.*

Curriculum-related talk prompts aim to scaffold the development of more formal or presentational language. They tend to include more sophisticated sentence structures, cohesive devices and may include key vocabulary. Talk prompts will look very different in different curriculum areas, e.g. a for-and-against talk prompt would particularly suit justification of opinions within a history topic. Examples include: *I think that. . .; I agree/ disagree with. . . because. . .; Other reasons include. . .; Also/additionally. . .; To conclude. . .*

On collaboration

'I usually buddy my beginner EAL learners with orally confident peers.'

Building on Vygotsky's theory of the Zone of Proximal Development (ZPD), well-constructed and collaborative tasks enable an EAL learner to perform at a higher level when supported by a linguistically more capable peer.

Pupils acquire language best, particularly academic language, through the context of the curriculum. Exploratory talk, where children construct new ideas and meanings through peer-talk, enables EAL learners to play around with curriculum-based informal language in a supportive non-threatening environment with plenty of opportunity for active listening, paraphrasing, recasting and repetition.

However, group work alone does not promote effective collaboration. To make group work genuinely collaborative and to create *thinking together* classrooms, teachers should:

- Take an active role in guiding their pupils' use of language and modelling expectations.
- Establish specific pupil roles within working groups, such as the 'recorder' (for specific task like timekeeping) or the 'clarifier' (particularly suitable for beginner EAL learners as it gives the pupil permission to ask questions about things they don't understand, thus supporting themselves as well as the rest of the group).
- Devise activities that promote shared knowledge, encourage debate and facilitate joint reasoning.

Collaborative approaches encourage pupils to think and work together within information-sharing contexts, and examples include processing and information-gap activities.

Teaching tip

With pupils, develop a set of agreed ground rules for collaboration and exploratory talk. Make these available as work cards and/or stick them on a prominent wall in each classroom.

Taking it further

Find out more about 'thinking together' approaches here: http://thinkingtogether.educ.cam.ac.uk.

Bonus idea ★

Visit the Collaborative Learning Project (www.collaborativelearning.org). This website contains numerous free talk-based curriculum-related activities that have been developed by practitioners over the last 30 years.

Cross-curricular drama

'Drama provides my EAL pupils with the chance to participate on a relatively equal footing with their peers. If they're not sure what to do, they can always pick up clues from watching and listening to others.'

The multimodal nature of drama makes it an effective tool for supporting the acquisition of oral skills, as well as for teaching learners about themselves and the wider world.

Teaching tip

Examples in different subjects include asking learners to behave like particles in liquid, encouraging learners to mark the moment of a story using freeze-frames, and organising the group into a human orchestra to produce a soundscape. For more ideas, visit: https://ealresources. bell-foundation.org.uk/ teachers/great-ideas-drama-and-role-play.

As an extra-curricular enterprise, drama can have significant benefits for all learners, but it can also have a huge impact when embedded across the curriculum and used in imaginative ways to consolidate learning. Drama offers a range of support for making meaning clear – visual, audio, kinaesthetic and practitioner modelling – in addition to the benefits of working collaboratively. Less confident EAL learners should perform relatively early but not first, so that they can learn from watching the first few groups; this helps to reinforce turn-taking and active listening. A whole-class dramatic technique can benefit new-to-English learners, as they can model themselves on others and avoid feeling too conspicuous.

The enhanced language demands of a more individualised strategy such as hot-seating may be more appropriate for advanced EAL learners. This requires learners to adopt the personality of a character or object. The learner in the hot seat needs as much information about the character as possible. The rest of the class develops suitable questions that the character or object in the hot seat answers, using imagination and building upon an understanding of the subject.

Bonus idea ★

Some theatre companies run specific workshops aimed at boosting the confidence and self-esteem of EAL learners, developing colloquial language along the way. Check online for local or national theatre companies that might be able to offer this service to your school.

Barrier games

'This is such a simple idea. Barrier games provide an authentic reason for peers to talk to each other.'

Barrier games are most effective when they develop academic language rooted in the curriculum.

Particularly useful for children and young people at the early stages of learning English, barrier games focus on developing speaking and listening skills. They help to develop instructional language, question starters, use of present tense, positional vocabulary, comparative terms, descriptive terminology and subject-specific language.

Typically, in barrier games, information is conveyed orally between two players, positioned either side of a physical barrier to prevent them from seeing an object that the other possesses. Ensure they can communicate easily, both orally and through non-verbal cues. One player provides a detailed description of a 'resource', which could be a drawing, object or sequence of items, selected from any subject or topic. The other player must recreate it as accurately as possible.

An alternative version has a pair of learners work collaboratively to piece together a complete visual resource from different versions that they both possess. Each learner takes turns to ask questions in order to obtain missing information about their resource. Questions focus on details such as size, position, shape, colour and written information such as text and numbers. Resources should be similar to each other but with a number of significant omissions (each of which must be visible on the other!). Appropriate resources include maps, diagrams, graphs, paintings, tables of information, timelines and even short texts.

Teaching tip

Sometimes it can be useful to pair learners up on either side of the barrier so they can discuss their questions and answers, especially if a beginner EAL learner is paired with an orally more proficient peer. A practitioner's input will also help keep participants on task.

Audio recording devices

'I like to record instructions and other useful information to give my EAL learners a degree of independence.'

Recording devices obviously help EAL learners to develop their speaking and listening skills. However, they also have tremendous potential for scaffolding writing.

Teaching tip

Pupils' oral recordings can be backed up and used to measure progress over time. Teachers can also leave oral feedback for learners – a real benefit for most children, whose listening skills tend to precede their reading proficiency. TalkingPENs and recordable sticky labels are particularly effective for this purpose (Idea 57).

Plan activities that require EAL learners to record a conversation, or their thoughts about an area of learning or a reading sample. Encourage pupils to listen to their recordings, look for errors and re-record if necessary. Use the recording function as a talk-for-writing approach where pairs and small groups can revisit conversations as a support for the writing process.

Recordable devices like *talking tins* or *talking postcards* are simple to use and have many applications across the curriculum. Not only can these devices record speech but also music, ambient sounds and other oral elements. Teachers and/or EAL learners can use them to develop treasure trails, create vocabulary prompts, design knowledge puzzles, support learning of phonemes and for practising word building or segmenting.

Bonus idea ★

Using a *talking photo album*, make up a book about how your school works. Include pertinent photographs and snippets of text and provide a voiceover in English and other languages. Leave this in the main office area so that parents can look and listen while waiting for an induction meeting.

Talking photo albums are perfect for linking visuals with audio elements. Use them to support new-arrival induction; learners can build personal scrapbooks or life stories using carefully selected printed images alongside recorded narration in L1 or English. They could develop talking books (Idea 44) from familiar stories or perhaps make a book about their new school. Alternatively, allow the new learner to use it as a diary to record thoughts and images during their first few weeks at school.

TalkingPEN (*PENpal*™)

'The look on Abdul's face when he heard the story in his language was priceless.'

PENpal™ is a pointing device that can play audio files when a user touches the tip of the pen to prepared hot spots on printed surfaces. There are many audio-enabled resources that work with the device, such as phonics materials, bilingual books and curriculum-related charts.

A great feature of TalkingPENs is that they can record audio and link the sound file to talking stickers that can be affixed to any surface, enabling practitioners to make bespoke resources for learners. Learners can also sound-enable their work and create talking games or exhibits.

As a practitioner, you could try making differentiated materials to scaffold learning at different levels, or leaving instructions, hints and key vocabulary on help cards, texts and worksheets to support a learning task. You can create support materials in L1 or leave oral feedback on work for learners who cannot read your comments. The pen can also be used to communicate with home or to make L1 oral translations of school forms to help with new-arrival induction.

In the hands of learners, the *PENpal*™ becomes the focus for speaking and listening activities. Allow beginner EAL learners to produce oral versions of work instead of writing if it is currently beyond their skill level. Develop activities for learners that require them to work together to develop sound-enabled products. Make a class *talking photo album* or yearbook, where the class can introduce itself to a new learner. Develop whole-school initiatives, such as creating an interactive talking display about the nationalities and language skills of all the learners and adults at the school.

Taking it further

Take a look at the pen-enabled resources available from Mantra Lingua. There are bilingual books, bilingual dictionaries, learning charts and phonics materials among many other resources (http://uk.mantralingua.com).

Bonus idea ★

Mantra Lingua provides a variety of additional free tools to enable schools to self-publish sound-enabled publications. Checkout *Youcreate* and *CreateLINK* (http://uk.mantralingua.com/content/software).

Talking avatars

'I have lots to say but am always too shy to stand up in front of everyone to do my presentation.'

Talking avatars encourage participation in oral activities, particularly those requiring a more formal register. Some of these tools are web-based while others are mobile apps, and many offer free functionality with additional features available for a small fee.

Teaching tip

Many talking avatar tools can be found for free on the internet and some cut-down versions of products such as *Crazy Talk* are occasionally distributed as free downloads with the cover price of a computer magazine.

Taking it further

Since finished versions can be stored as evidence, talking avatars can be used to assess speaking and listening. It may also be useful to compare presentations produced at the beginning of the year and at the end in order to show progress over time.

These digital tools allow a user to utilise an animated character (avatar) that can 'read' text aloud or 'speak' it from an audio recording. Users can change the background or look of their avatar and choose from a range of synthesised voices. Apps like *Morfo* allow the in-built camera to capture and use real faces, animating them on screen to accompany the audio component.

A natural starting point might be to use the system's text-to-speech voice synthesiser. Working on individual or collaboratively developed texts, the user types or pastes text into the system and chooses a voice. Hearing good-quality audio rendering of the text provides an effective model, helping learners to spot mistakes and rehearse for their own recordings. Talking avatars are useful for preparing learners for oral presentations such as show and tell or public speaking. *Voki* allows users to record an oral version away from the computer and import it into the system at a later time. Provide a quiet space and portable recording equipment for this. Some learners will want privacy, while others may appreciate the presence of supportive peers. Another way of preparing the audio is to attach a microphone to the computer and record directly into the software. When the audio has been linked to the avatar, the whole presentation can be exported and saved to a website, blog or virtual learning environment.

Opinion lines

'Opinion line debating is an excellent way to help pupils prepare for argumentative/persuasive writing. The emphasis on academic talk has particular resonance for more advanced EAL learners.'

The open-ended nature of this type of activity encourages pupils to experiment with language and take more risks as they seek to justify their chosen position along a continuum. The quality and quantity of academic talk successfully models the process and usually converts into better writing.

A simple version of the technique requires you to pose a question or statement that is likely to promote a range of views in the class. In small groups, encourage learners to come to a consensus about where to place the question or statement along an opinion line continuum (from 'strongly agree' to 'strongly disagree').

Once positioned, ask someone from one group to indicate where they placed it along the opinion line and justify their decision. Encourage the rest of the class to offer supportive comments or counter-arguments where appropriate. Modelling and talk prompt sheets (Idea 52) can help with scaffolding oral contributions.

This activity also works well with multiple statements around a particular theme. Allocate each group a different statement or allow them to choose their own.

In a suitable room, you might like to run the activity more kinaesthetically, first posing one or more questions or statements. Representatives can stand by one of five opinion signs on the walls, justifying their chosen position. The rest of the class can support or counter-argue where necessary, with the representative moving to a new position if they change their mind.

Bonus idea ★
Washing lines provide a way for children to give their personal opinion over a more prolonged period of time where their opinion might change from day to day. Hung across the classroom, a child can move their name along a washing line according to their individual perception about a particular issue. Each name could be pinned up with a *Recordable Talking Peg* so that a pupil can add a short oral recording to justify their thinking (see www.tts-group. co.uk/recordable- talking-pegs-assorted- colours/1002408.html).

Reading and viewing

Part 6

Use of bilingual books

'It was so heartening to see Gabriella's eyes light up when she saw her language in a book provided by her teacher.'

Sourcing and using high-quality bilingual books sends a clear message to pupils and parents about the school's commitment to maintaining the first languages of the whole school community.

Find out how one local authority, London Borough of Redbridge, set up a home–school bilingual reading project. Entitled *Developing reading skills through home languages*, the project produced teaching and classroom resources along with a project booklet. It also includes helpful guidance on engaging parents.

Project details: www.rnlcom.com/ the-networks/pupil-mobilitynew-arrivals

Direct link to project booklet (pdf): www. rnlcom.com/wp-content/ uploads/2015/02/ Developing-reading-skills-through-home-languages.pdf

Remembering that not all EAL learners or parents are literate in L1, bilingual texts can have a significant role to play in activating a learner's prior knowledge, as well as supporting their access to the curriculum. Practitioners will also benefit from access to age-appropriate bilingual books in order to facilitate first language reading assessments (Idea 13).

For new-to-English learners, a bilingual storybook provides instant access to a story that can inform subsequent literacy tasks, whether in English or another language. Bilingual learners beyond the early stages of learning English will benefit from exposure to both texts at the same time. Sometimes, try covering one of the texts or particular words or phrases for more active reading. In this way, bilingual learners will be able to transfer knowledge over from L1 to English and vice versa.

All learners, including monolingual English speakers, will benefit from being able to see two different scripts on the same page. Get groups to compare specific elements such as text directionality, word breaks and punctuation, and ask them to identify root words that may be common to the two languages.

Get the family involved by developing guidance for parents about how to share a book with their child and translate it into the main community languages.

Choosing appropriate books/ reading schemes

'When I see older English beginners being taught to read from "picture books", it makes me really angry.'

Choosing appropriate reading material can be extremely challenging. It is all too easy to choose texts that are too demanding or ones that are simplistic and demeaning to the age and cognitive ability of the EAL learner.

Ensure that books are age-appropriate and well-produced, with clear fonts and engaging illustrations that add contextual meaning. Stories with strong narratives or familiar non-fiction topics will be more appealing than texts without an authentic purpose. Similarly, learners are more likely to engage with texts that relate to their own experiences, reflect the society in which they live and deal with issues of culture and religion sensitively, challenging bias and stereotype where necessary.

While phonics are an important part of helping most children to learn to read, including EAL learners, 'phonics books' that build stories around set sounds may not be the most engaging texts to expose children to at the early stages of learning English.

Digital books are generally supportive as they often include professionally recorded narration and/or offer text-to-speech rendering through the hosting device (Idea 68). Being able to change the reading speed and the type of voice and word highlighting are helpful features. Many digital books incorporate contextual glossaries that provide instant word definitions. Some even allow you to play around inside the story by adding your own voice narration.

Teaching tip

Try to select stories that are written with an active voice. This will be more accessible to EAL learners, who will mostly be drawing from their experiences in oral communication. Avoid texts that are overly colloquial, as this type of language tends to lie outside the experience of many EAL learners, particularly beginners. Where texts contain an abundance of academic and technical language, choose those that provide a glossary.

Reading miscue analysis

'When I sat down and spent 30 minutes listening to Pavel reading, I realised that he had all the relevant strategies in place.'

EAL learners may get low reading ages in tests because of limited vocabulary rather than their inability to decode fluently.

Late beginner EAL learners and early advanced learners are found to have reading ages that are lower than chronological age, as assessed through a standardised reading test. However, these tests can be highly unreliable because of differences in wider cultural understanding.

For readers who are not fully fluent, it can be helpful to listen to them in their L1 to gauge fluency and confidence before assessing decoding and self-correction ability in English. Miscue analysis is a systematic technique for recording a reader's strengths, supporting the practitioner to choose books at the appropriate levels and set appropriate targets.

1. Ask the learner to pick a reading book they think they can read quite well. Photocopy a couple of pages so you also have a copy.
2. Give them time to read through a page silently first, then ask the pupil to read aloud.
3. While the pupil is reading, tick every correct word, writing the 'miscues' over any mistakes.
4. You need to use an agreed set of codes for miscues, e.g. 'SC' for self-correction. There are lots of ready-made templates available online.
5. At the end of the session, add up the mistakes in the different categories to give you a clear learning target. A pupil may make lots of mistakes pronouncing medial vowels, or constantly guess the words they cannot read, but get the right grammatical form.

Understanding multimodality

'My KS2 science revision book is really hard to understand. There are so many pictures and diagrams; I don't know which parts are important.'

Most school textbooks and online reading materials include data, pictures and other visuals, which also need to be 'read' and interpreted.

Multimodal literacy, first proposed by Professors Gunter Kress and Carey Jewitt, involves understanding the diverse ways we have of making meaning, including the written word, spoken language, gesture and images. These are our semiotic resources and can be found in a variety of media.

It can be difficult for learners from cultures where visual imagery is not commonly used in education to understand how we interpret multimodal texts such as advertisements, posters and websites.

Teachers need to make explicit:

- How bold/italicised fonts, underlining and colour add to the meanings created by the written word, e.g. for emphasis, to indicate entry in a glossary or to highlight where there is a hyperlink in a digital text.
- How information texts lay out content via titles, topic sentences and paragraphs and how this can be useful to extract meaning.
- Where captions or explanations for key visuals or photographic sources tend to appear (to the left or below) in comparison to titles for tabulated data and graphs (above).
- How information such as asterisks or footnote numbers can be signposted via superscript.
- The meaning of digital writing cues such as red underlining in word-processed documents.

Teaching tip

Collect a range of printed/digital examples of stylistic conventions used in multimodal texts. Put them all together in a folder or embed them in a *PowerPoint* presentation. Annotate them to make explicit what pupils need to be aware of in order to extract as much meaning as possible.

Taking it further

Exams usually include multimodal texts, so go over exam question conventions with children – emphasis for important words, number of marks available, where to write the answer, etc.

Use graphic texts

'Most children love cartoons and I find them a great way to develop the wider reading skills of my beginner EAL learners.'

Graphic texts present fiction and non-fiction through a more visual cartoon style than traditional books do. The text tends to be less dense, more informal and supported visually through images and stylistic conventions that help convey meaning. Many also contain vocabulary and grammar activities linked to the text. This makes them perfect for early readers.

Many EAL learners, including those from abroad, may be familiar with a cartoon-style such as manga. However, it is still important to explain some of the more immediate conventions, such as reading directionality; how text is organised to imply narrative, thoughts and speech; and the meaning of onomatopoeic expressions, ellipses and other unusual punctuation.

Visual cues can also be confusing. You could prepare learners by asking them to think of ways to visually communicate ideas such as speed, an unpleasant smell or heat without any words.

Ideas for developing active reading include:

- Text marking – identify time-based cohesive devices, setting description, imperative verbs and so on.
- Cloze procedure – blank out individual words that need to be predicted.
- Text reconstruction – remove chunks of text from narrative panes or speech or thought bubbles, and ask learners to rewrite small sections using their own words.
- Story sequence – provide a scrambled set of panes that require sequencing to retell the story.
- Comic jigsaw – separate all the text from the images and ask learners to recombine them correctly.

Bonus idea ★

Blank out the text in the commentary boxes or thought/speech bubbles of a graphic text or comic and ask the pupils to rewrite the story.

Word building and morphology (Latin and Greek)

'Now I know why bilingual means speaking two languages — "bi" means "two" and comes from Latin.'

Approximately 80% of the vocabulary of mathematics, science and technical English derives from Latin or Greek (often via French).

EAL learners are generally more metalinguistically aware than their monolingual peers, due to their knowledge of one or more languages beyond English. Those with L1 related to Romance languages have an advantage here. Reinforcing pupils' understanding of Greek and Latin roots/suffixes will help them make informed guesses about the meanings of new words.

Meaning	Greek	Latin	Examples
1	mono	uni	monotone, unicycle
2	di	bi, duo	dioxide, bicycle, duet
3	tri	tri	triangle, tripod
4	tetra	quad (quart)	tetrahedron, quadrilateral
5	pent	quint	pentagon, quintet
6	hex	sext	hexagon, sextet
8	octo	octo	octagon, octave
10	deca	deci	decade, decimal
100	(hecto)	cent	centurion, cents
1000	kilo	mille	kilometre, millennium
half	hemi	semi	hemisphere, semicolon
many	poly	multi	polygon, multiply

Word clouds

'Word clouds are perfect for drilling down to topic vocabulary because all the common words can be removed from a text, leaving behind the most important keywords.'

Word clouds can be produced by online tools/apps; they enable a user to produce a cluster of words based on the frequency of words in a digital text (including words in different languages). This technique has many applications for teachers working with EAL learners, particularly those who are at more advanced stages of learning English.

Teaching tip

Let pupils make their own word clouds to consolidate their learning of topic vocabulary. Encourage them to edit their word lists and also to play around with the font style and colour scheme as this will teach them about media literacy. Finished word clouds provide ready-made assessment opportunities for teachers since they can be printed or saved for future viewing.

Suggested online word cloud tools include *Wordle* (www.wordle.net) and *Wordsift* (www. wordsift.com).

The ability to visually produce word clouds, where the size of each word indicates how frequently it appears in a text, is particularly supportive of language learning because it can focus attention on:

- subject-specific vocabulary and academic process words/phrases
- tense
- cohesive devices
- the interconnectedness of related words.

Here are some ideas for how teachers and learners can use word clouds both in the classroom and during home learning:

- At the beginning of a new piece of work, try producing a word cloud from a topic summary or essay that covers the salient points; learners can pick out some of the key vocabulary and check the meaning if needed. Ask them to predict the genre and text type that the text has been drawn from.
- Topic word clouds can be used as quick revision guides.

- Opinion-based texts can be studied using this technique in order to support learners' understanding of the particular position taken by the author.
- Two or more word clouds can be compared in order to demonstrate how word usage changes according to era, genre, text type and so on.
- Personal writing can be analysed in order to support redrafting, e.g. by showing how lower-level writing might have an overabundance of certain verbs, adjectives or common conjunctions such as 'and'. (You may need to change the settings in the word cloud program to allow what it labels as 'common words' to be displayed, as the default setting may automatically remove these words from the final output.)

Bonus idea ★

Try using word cloud programs such as *Wordart.com* as this allows a user to wrap the text inside an appropriate shape to add visual pizazz to their word clouds.

DARTs

'My EAL learners usually read very passively, focusing more on decoding than anything else.'

Directed Activities Related to Texts (DARTs) are designed to challenge learners to engage with texts by using active reading strategies. Some DARTs help learners to consider the overall structure of a text, while others focus on supporting understanding and interpretation. Choosing the right one to meet the learning needs of the pupils is critical. They can be used effectively across the curriculum with both fiction and non-fiction texts.

Teaching tip

When working with texts from a number of different sources, marking words or phrases in different colours can help organise ideas and language conceptually, prior to repurposing text into a different format. Once text is categorised, provide learners with graphic organisers (Idea 39); this will help them to partially process chunks of language before transforming it into, say, a letter, newspaper article or advertisement.

Taking it further

Further examples of DARTs can be found here: http://teachit.so/index_htm_files/DARTs.pdf.

Sometimes EAL learners need access to a modified version of a text for practical reasons, such as its length and complexity, while other DARTs work best with unmodified texts. To improve writing structure, get learners to demarcate one long paragraph that has no full stops or ask learners to break up an unformatted piece of text using headings, sub-headings and topic sentences.

Another useful strategy is to ask learners to mark important words in preparation for further tasks. Examples include highlighting 'weak' verbs in order to identify where to use more 'powerful' ones or, in argument writing, highlighting all the cohesive devices and choosing more suitable words to mark where additional points are being made as opposed to making counter-arguments. Reconstruction DARTS include text completion (cloze, word/phrase substitution, top and tail sentences), sequencing jumbled segments of text, grouping chunks of text into categories, prediction (writing the next step), and dictogloss (Idea 75). Analysis DARTS include text marking, sorting or ranking information/statements, annotating a living graph and breaking text into categories (e.g. paragraph headings, topic sentences).

Rendering text to speech

'Hearing a text read aloud enhances understanding and can also help develop reading skills.'

Most EAL learners demonstrate greater proficiency with spoken English than they do with reading and writing. Digital devices and integrated software can read text aloud, enabling learners to access written information that would be otherwise inaccessible.

Early readers benefit from text-to-speech in situations where a lot of curriculum knowledge needs to be communicated through text; this enables participation in subsequent activities that require learners to have internalised the required information.

It's a good idea to have screen readers installed on various computers around the school. Some versions work within word processors and web browsers, while others allow text to be pasted from the clipboard. There are also portable versions that need no installation and can be accessed directly from a memory stick. Software and online tools can also take a text file and convert it into an audio file. In this way, text can be made more accessible both in the lesson and for a more blended approach where pupils can pre-listen to content prior to the lesson.

Experiment by choosing appropriately synthesised voices and other software settings. Some applications allow a user to change the speed of oral reading; this can assist learners with differing linguistic and cognitive abilities. It may also be possible to set up the software to highlight text as it is read aloud; doing this helps to reinforce word recognition.

Teaching tip

The text-to-speech facility is integrated into all modern mobile devices such as phones and tablets and can be set up easily from within 'settings' on each device.

Living graphs

'When we did *Holes*, I found it easy to know how tension changed in the book from the graph.'

Living graphs are graphs or charts that use textual annotations to help pupils interpret what is happening at specific data points. They can also be used as a bridge to writing.

Analysing and evaluating data is a form of higher-order thinking that is difficult for some EAL learners to fully express through writing. An explanatory text needs a specific structure and utilises cause-and-effect language and a range of technical vocabulary pertinent to different subject areas. Use 'living graphs' to help learners interpret trends and patterns in data that have been obtained through their own investigations or with graphs/charts drawn from pre-existing data. Living graphs require learners to justify the position of information against a timeline of events.

In preparation, create a variety of true statements that help to describe and explain the overall shape of the graph. Try to include ambiguous or irrelevant information as this encourages active reading. Produce a set of cards containing all the statements, and encourage learners to place them in appropriate positions on the graph. Encourage the group to discard any irrelevant or untrue statements.

Living graphs can be developed around any kind of continuous data, such as:

- a bar graph showing how the volume of traffic varies over the course of a day
- a seismograph of earth movements before, during and after an earthquake

Bonus idea ★

Free web-based tools are available to make living graphs – here are a couple to get you started:

ReadWriteThink – www.readwritethink.org/classroom-resources/student-interactives/graphic-30039.html.

ClassTools.net – www.classtools.net/education-games-php/livingGraph.

- a population pyramid illustrating population demographics over time
- a tension graph showing how a character's emotions vary over time (fiction or non-fiction)
- a line graph describing the interrelationship between a predator and its prey over a number of years.

Once the position of the statements has been agreed, learners can sequence them to form a detailed, cohesive piece of writing, e.g. an explanation of the flow of traffic throughout the day.

Taking it further

Pupils can learn a lot from annotating or making their own living graphs. Pupils could add annotations to significant data points on a pre-existing graph or chart; create their own graph/chart and add annotations; or create a graph, produce a set of card annotations and ask peers to place these cards onto the graph/chart in the correct positions.

Supporting writing

Part 7

Using writing frames

'I never know how to start; it's the most hard part of writing.'

There is a place for writing frames to be used with both beginner and more advanced EAL learners. However, they are unlikely to help new-to-English learners, who need to concentrate first on developing their speaking and listening skills. Additionally, think carefully about their use with more able writers, as they can limit or confine the finished piece.

Develop simple frames for beginner learners who find it hard to start or sustain writing beyond a couple of sentences. Distil the scope of the frame to a few key sentences, and provide starter words and phrases to help scaffold the writing. Imagine that you require an account of a class trip to the local zoo. An appropriate frame might look something like this:

To start with. . .
Then. . .
Next. . .
After that. . .
Finally. . .

More advanced learners tend to write quite well, but they may have trouble with organising their work or they may be reluctant to take risks with different types of phrases and cohesive devices. Prepare more complex templates that offer the user a choice of words or phrases to scaffold their writing. Organise the frame into different sections to highlight how to organise the different elements of the text. Writing text types such as discussion, explanation and persuasion can be particularly difficult for some learners, and writing frames can help with this. For more information and suggestions, Maureen Lewis and David Wray have produced a number of useful publications connected with writing frames (see References and further reading).

Bonus idea ★

Perhaps learners have been researching a topic and need to write a persuasive letter. A frame to support the bulk of the letter could be laid out in this way:

Your view: *I think that/ My view is. . .*

Your reasons: *The main reason is. . . because . . . Also. . . Moreover/ Additionally. . . Finally. . .*

Concluding the letter: *To sum up/To conclude, I would like. . . An acceptable solution/ compromise would/ might/could be. . .*

Topic mats

'Having access to topic information and technical vocabulary gives both beginner and more advanced EAL learners real confidence in their writing.'

Topic mats can be as simple as a vocabulary list or as sophisticated as an infographic or mind map. While potentially useful throughout a unit of work, judicial use for specific writing activities can enhance their impact.

At their simplest, topic mats feature words and images associated with a particular topic. Older or more advanced learners will benefit from charts containing specific language to assist with thinking and talking around a topic, as well as supporting academic writing.

It's important that this kind of resource looks 'professional'. Cluster similar types of language in boxes, and use plenty of little diagrams and symbols to reinforce meaning. The specific content on each chart will obviously vary according to subject area and the specific topic. Content might include small maps, timelines, graphs, diagrams and models. Language elements might be organised in any of the following ways:

- technical vocabulary related to the topic
- process words, e.g. *discuss, describe, explain, compare, evaluate*
- context-related information, e.g. names of objects, places, characters or the like
- descriptive language related to the context/ topic
- comparative terms
- frequently-used cohesive devices.

Teaching tip

Try producing A3 laminated versions. It can help to leave a relatively sparse area in the centre of the mat where a learner can place a book or piece of paper yet still be able to see the main content.

Develop graphic texts

'My beginners really enjoy filling in boxes and bubbles with snippets of text and short phrases. It helps them overcome the fear of a blank piece of paper and builds their confidence.'

Graphic texts require a limited amount of writing and are perfect for bridging the gap to more extensive pieces. It will help EAL learners if texts are directly linked to work they are currently undertaking within the mainstream curriculum.

Teaching tip

Graphic texts can easily be enhanced by adding an oral component. An oral component could use L1, English or a combination of the two.

Taking it further

Add sound to printed graphic texts using Mantra Lingua's *PENpal*™ and talking stickers (Idea 57).

Bonus idea ★

Using digital cameras, encourage groups to take freeze-frame photographs of themselves in appropriate settings and import them into the software alongside other digital images.

Getting learners involved in producing their own graphic texts is a creative way of supporting writing across the curriculum. The graphical layout acts as a storyboard around which formal description, narrative and informal speech-bubble dialogue can be constructed.

For printed versions, photocopy the relevant sections and obscure the text within the narrative boxes and speech or thought bubbles. For digital versions, take screenshots and edit out the relevant sections of text. The images can then be imported into a word processor, desktop publishing program or presentation package ready for learners to type in their own texts.

There are many useful software packages that allow you to create graphic texts from scratch. Some, like *Kar2ouche* (http://creativeedutech.com/products/kar2ouche), contain banks of curriculum-related materials – settings, characters, props, text boxes – that can be stitched together, while other software, like *Comic Life* (http://plasq.com), is perfect for building graphic texts using real photographs. Learners can choose from a range of graphic templates, add legends, speech or thought bubbles and develop narrative-based texts. *Book Creator* is a user-friendly word processing app that contains a simple cartoon template to assist production of graphic texts.

Embedding grammar

'In my experience, grammar has to be taught in context else it doesn't become sticky learning.'

Research into the writing of EAL learners (Cameron, 2003) shows that less successful writers tend to fall down on specific grammatical elements, particularly the correct use of adverbials, modal verbs, prepositions, subject–verb agreement and verb tenses and endings.

Each school will need to consider the best approaches for the teaching of grammar to EAL learners. Learners acquire language most successfully in the context of the curriculum rather than through decontextualised drills or vocabulary exercises, so any focus on grammar should link directly to ongoing topics within the mainstream curriculum; especially if children are in withdrawal contexts. The tendency to jump around a lot between genres and text types for the purposes of preparing for the spelling and grammar component of the KS2 SATs will be challenging for EAL learners, particularly those who are relatively new to English. Where possible, try to cover aspects of grammar within sequences of lessons where context is clear and the knowledge component has been explicitly covered.

Substitution tables are a useful grammatical technique that help teachers highlight grammatical forms used in different subject areas. Here is an example within science:

I found out that	iron plastic steel paper copper	was / was not	attracted by the magnet

Taking it further

The 2002 National Strategies *Grammar for Writing* materials can be used to address specific aspects of grammar for advanced EAL learners. The materials come with a useful set of *Clicker* grids that can be used to support text-construction exercises using pictures and speech (DfES, 2002).

Bonus idea

Language Garden (www.languagegarden. com) has been successfully used with EAL learners to help them develop a greater variety of sentence structures during creative writing. Using the metaphor of a growing plant, colourful branching stories can be built up in stages, modelling the differing purposes for verbs, adjectives, prepositions and so on.

Blogs and tweets

'My advanced EAL learners like *Twitter* because everyone is restricted to a limited number of characters; they say it makes them feel the same as everyone else.'

Getting learners involved in blogging is an excellent way of linking reading and writing, as well as developing learners' media-literacy skills. It also encourages pupils to think carefully about their audience.

Try to devise blogging activities that require learners to write about issues either from their own point of view or in a more factual, impartial way. Encourage learners to read each other's blogs and add their own comments, as this can be highly motivating for them.

Twitter's ease of use and restriction on message length is popular among educators working with learners acquiring English. By its very nature, Twitter requires learners to think about the formality of their communication, as well as about how to write concisely.

It makes sense to set up a unique *Twitter* account just for use with a particular group or class of learners. Using this account, you will be able to initiate many different kinds of collaborative reading and writing tasks, including:

- researching definitions of new words through a 'word of the week' activity
- writing a summary of the last lesson
- improving a sentence by changing or adding just one word at a time
- building a collaborative story by taking turns to contribute to it
- tweeting from the perspective of a historical character or celebrity
- organising a poll or vote about a specific subject.

Bonus idea ★

Using an app like *TextingStory* (available on iOS and Android), pupils can fake an imaginary text-based conversation between two individuals; this appears like a text conversation on a phone's screen or tablet device. This is a fun way to restrict the quantity of writing and could be used to develop content-rich fictionalised texts within any topic area.

Dictogloss

'This is my number one idea for developing the writing of more advanced EAL learners.'

Dictogloss links active listening, note taking, writing and reading within any curriculum area. It supports the acquisition of different types of language including key vocabulary, typical phrases and cohesive devices that are distinctive to particular text types.

In a dictogloss activity, a text is read several times to learners working in small groups. As the text is read out loud, pupils make notes about what they hear in a graphic organiser (Idea 39). Finally, each group writes a similar but not identical version of the original text. Ensure each group has a mixture of EAL learners and orally proficient English speakers. While this may sound like dictation, be assured that it is not the same at all!

1. Read the text aloud at normal speed and encourage each group to listen without taking notes. Then ask them to briefly explain the gist of the text.
2. Read the text a second time, slightly more slowly; allow learners to take notes with an emphasis on more obvious elements, like facts and specific vocabulary.
3. Read the text a third time; pupils should continue note taking, but this time devote more attention to specific phrases and cohesive devices that link ideas together.
4. Allow 10 to 15 minutes for the groups to piece together as much of the text as possible.

Choose several groups to read their collaboratively developed texts aloud and draw out specific points, such as which elements were easy or difficult to recreate. This should help inform a focus for future work.

Teaching tip

The chosen text needs to be relatively short and should focus upon specific content and language elements that you wish to reinforce. It is essential to provide the participants with a note-taking graphic organiser that suits the text type.

Taking it further

Read more about dictogloss here in the DCSF's *CPDM 5: Bridging talk and text* (2009). Available at: www.naldic.org.uk/Resources/NALDIC/Teaching%20and%20Learning/CPDM5.pdf.

Vocabulary development

'Emre's scientific knowledge is way ahead of his peers. But his lack of vocabulary really frustrates him because he can't fully express what he knows.'

Learning lots of words could be a pointless activity unless it genuinely supports wider academic learning. Vocabulary should be developed within the clear context of the ongoing curriculum, whether this is pre-learning at home, pre-taught in short-term withdrawal situations or within the mainstream curriculum.

Taking it further

Use technology to assist in easy development of vocabulary games. *Osric's Bingo Card Generator* is a web-based tool that enables easy production of uniquely different bingo cards. There are two versions – one uses words only and the other allows the use of images (www.osric.com/bingo-card-generator and www.osric.com/bingo-card-generator/images.html).

The following are a few ideas for reinforcing and recapping recently acquired language.

- Prepare a set of 'connection cards' ready for a language-based starter activity. Connection cards are matching pairs, e.g. vocabulary and definitions, top and tail sentences, cause and effect statements. Give learners a connection card each, and encourage them to find the pupil who holds the matching card. At the end of a set time period, get each learner pair to read out their matched cards to check that they are correct.

- 'Follow me' is an oral version of connection cards, played by the whole class, that is particularly useful for learners who are beginning to read, as the activity has a simple script from which to work. Each learner is given one card; the idea is that one learner starts by reading out the card, which might say something such as 'I have a square, how many lines of symmetry do I have?'. In this case, the learner with the card that says 'I have four; tell me another shape with four right angles' should read it out, and so on. Each card should have only one following card to avoid any confusion.

- A bingo starter activity is an excellent way to recap key language in preparation for the main lesson activity. Create a set of bingo

cards based upon key vocabulary and a set
of definitions to read out during the bingo
activity. Play the game until someone 'wins'.
Go through each definition to ensure the
keywords are matched correctly.

- 'Vocabulary *Jenga*®' is another great idea.
Target vocabulary is written on the underside
of *Jenga*® bricks covered in masking tape.
The game proceeds as normal between two
teams but as a brick is removed, the player
must either define the word or perhaps place
the word into a meaningful sentence. If all
agree that they have got it correct, the player
asks someone on the other team to place
the brick onto the *Jenga*® tower. However, if
the player gets it wrong then they must place
it onto the tower, incurring the risk of the
tower collapsing.

- 'Topic taboo' is based on a commercially
available card game. Each card features
a topic word/phrase and a number of
'forbidden' words/phrases written below.
Playing in teams, a pupil has to describe their
word/phrase to their team without using any
of the 'forbidden' words. It's a good idea to
allow pupils to make their own cards too and
then play their game in teams.

- To recap learning at the end of a lesson, try
the 'Generation game' activity. Prepare a
PowerPoint visual containing all the language
elements and other information relevant
to a particular topic. This can be setup in a
number of ways. Convey each idea on its
own slide using appropriate text, images
and sounds. Set the presentation to play
automatically, so that each slide remains on
screen for a set amount of time before giving
way to the next. Alternatively, set a number
of images to cross a slide one by one using
the animation feature in *PowerPoint*. When
the presentation is over, ask learners to try
to remember as many pieces of language or
information as possible.

Digital writing tools

'In my language, we write from the right; these new letters are hard for me.'

These tools contain a number of in-built supports for writing. However, for EAL learners, some tools will be more appropriate than others. Used inappropriately, certain tools used by emergent writers can be more confusing than helpful, while more advanced learners may come to rely on tools that they don't actually need. Correct use of each tool needs to be specifically taught.

Modern technology can greatly speed up the process of getting text into an editable format. Not only can you use cameras to photograph print and convert it into digital text, but the listening mode on devices allows a user to speak in real time and capture their speech accurately within the software/app of choice. Slow writers and those unfamiliar with keyboards or touch-screen keyboards (soft keyboards) will really appreciate this shortcut.

For those at an earlier stage of learning English

- Learners who are newer to English often worry a lot about the number of errors they make, as indicated by the spelling and grammar-checking feature, so it can be a good idea to turn off real-time error checking. Moreover, the conventions of green and red underlining will be meaningless to the user unless they are clearly explained.
- The 'auto-correct' feature may be helpful because it seamlessly corrects a whole raft of basic errors. Being free from the worry of making simple errors can help less confident writers focus on the more immediate task of constructing cohesive texts.

- Soft keyboard word prediction will only be useful for those children who are beginning to read independently.
- The thesaurus will probably be unhelpful to early beginners, as it may refer learners to too many unfamiliar or new words.
- Text-to-speech technology (Idea 68) can help with self-correction because it enables learners to hear back what they have written and more easily spot their mistakes.
- For learners who have developed some oral competency, as already mentioned, speech-to-text can speed up the process of writing digitally (but children must not become over-reliant on this approach).

For more advanced learners
- These learners will appreciate having access to real-time spelling and grammar checking, as this will help them identify their mistakes and give them the option to make corrections.
- The thesaurus will be more useful to advanced learners, as they have a wider vocabulary and thus will be able to make more informed choices about which words to vary in their writing.
- Soft keyboards will help with in-word prediction, as well as between words for thinking about the next word (based upon collocation principles).
- Be aware that overreliance on writing support tools can mask systematic errors or hide more serious problems.

Taking it further

OneNote, from Microsoft Office, has the capability to convert print into digital text via OCR. Handwriting drawn onto a touch screen can also be converted into digital text.

Supportive word processors

'I like hearing back what I have written. It helps me check my work.'

Clicker Docs, **a supportive word processor produced by Cricksoft, is particularly useful for emergent writers because it contains a number of powerful supports for writing. The software is highly configurable; the level of support can be matched to each learner's needs.**

Taking it further

Sign up to *LearningGrids*, an online repository for plugin resources for Clicker apps. These resources have been prepared by practitioners to support writing across the curriculum (www. learninggrids.com/uk).

To illustrate how *Clicker Docs* can be used, consider Ivan, a Year 2 EAL learner, who has been studying English for well over a year. He has been asked to write a couple of short paragraphs about The Great Fire of London.

Ivan has access to a simplified keyboard. Once he has written his first sentence, the in-built text-to-speech synthesis automatically plays back his writing, providing him with an authentic oral model and assisting him with error checking. The red underlining focuses his attention on incorrectly spelled words; by touching the word, he automatically gets access to a list of alternative words that are also audio-enabled. Ivan notices that below the text entry area, words begin to appear in a list as he types. This word prediction has been enabled by his teacher, allowing him to quickly select the word he needs from a list and paste it into his writing. For his next sentence, he is presented with words that naturally appear at a sentence's beginning, and when he needs a specific grammatical construction, a list of appropriate words becomes available. Ivan also uses a topic word bar, set up by his teacher, presenting a set of alphabetically ordered words and phrases that help Ivan with connecting ideas together. The word bar has also been organised into sections like 'before the fire' and 'the fire starts', providing Ivan with additional support for structuring his final piece.

Bonus idea ★

Check out the other apps in the *Clicker* series, including *Clicker Sentences, Clicker Books* and *Clicker Connect.*

Promoting an intercultural dimension

Part 8

Running a dual-language storytelling session

'Sofia loved reading *The Giant Turnip* to us in Russian. She was very proud that it originated from her country.'

Running a dual-language storytelling session is a perfect way to involve bilingual adults and children from the whole school community.

Teaching tip

Collect a range of resources to support the storytelling session, such as dressing-up clothes, props, musical instruments and puppets. Suitable music can enrich the experience for the audience, and it may be possible to play an eBook or project images from a book via an IWB. Alternatively, accompany the storytelling with a piece of drama created by the pupils.

Try auditing the bilingual skills of practitioners, learners and parents, in order to identify suitable volunteers to participate in a storytelling session. You may be able to source bilingual adults from key workers in the local authority, and it is also possible to hold a story session over a videoconferencing link (Idea 92).

Choose stories that build upon the languages and traditions of the major communities attending the school. Hearing different languages used within formal situations will raise the status of EAL pupils and enrich the lives of all learners.

Suitable opportunities for a bilingual storytelling session might include:

- welcoming a new learner to the school
- preparing for a digital storytelling project (Idea 45)
- celebrating a religious festival
- supporting a cultural event like Gypsy Roma Traveller Month
- promoting an international event such as European Day of Languages or Refugee Week
- keeping up the momentum of The Young Interpreter Scheme® (Idea 97).

Bonus idea ★

Try recording a live session (or one delivered via VC) and showcase it via the school's website.

Ideally, you should read or retell the first section of the story in the other language and then alternate with English throughout.

Cross-cultural mathematics

'It was really interesting to learn that in the Chinese culture the number eight is considered to be lucky.'

The contribution of different cultures to the development of mathematics through the ages is a tremendous learning opportunity for all children.

Looking at mathematics from a geographical and historical perspective can greatly contribute to the development of an intercultural dimension within the curriculum, while providing an opportunity for EAL learners to demonstrate knowledge and skill in mathematics from their own linguistic or cultural background that might otherwise be ignored. Here are some ideas for activities:

- Investigate the contributions of people from across the world to the development of mathematics, e.g. early Muslim Arabic scholars and Indian mathematicians.
- Learn about some famous 'discoveries', e.g. the use of zero as a placeholder and the golden ratio.
- Investigate the importance of specific numbers to some cultures, e.g. lucky and unlucky numbers.
- Practise counting to ten in different languages.
- Learn how to write numerals and numbers in different number systems, ancient and modern, or find out about different base systems – binary (2), Mayan (20), Babylonian (60) and others.
- Research counting and calculating equipment from around the world, e.g. the abacus, quipu or Napier's rods.
- Identify different ways of solving mathematical problems, e.g. Egyptian, Gelosia and grid multiplication.

Taking it further

Build up a bank of resources to enrich different areas of the school: posters of famous mathematicians for the library; different currencies, menus and product labels for role-play areas; board games like *Go*, *Mancala* and *Carrom* to play during wet breaks or 'golden time'.

Bonus idea ★

You could also look at some of the interesting connections between mathematics and other subjects such as art, music and architecture, or discover where mathematical words have come from, e.g. 'algebra', 'circle' and 'centre'.

Language of the month

'I enjoyed teaching my friends the numbers from one to ten in Hindi. Even my teacher joined in.'

Many schools choose to celebrate the plurilingual nature of their community by focusing on a different language each month during the academic year. This is an excellent way of drawing upon the language skills of the EAL population and boosting their self-esteem.

While this type of enrichment activity is beneficial for schools with a large ethnic minority population, it is worth mentioning that all schools need to consider different ways of celebrating diversity and promoting an intercultural dimension, both in and out of the mainstream curriculum.

Here are some suggested activities:

- Have learners answer the register in the target language.
- Create a display featuring the chosen language. Use audio devices like *talking tins* and TalkingPENs to bring the display alive orally.
- Host an assembly about the language of the month.
- Conduct language taster sessions; where possible, this should involve EAL learners and their parents.
- Prepare a library box with relevant resources, e.g. bilingual books, dual-language dictionaries, etc.
- Record audio and video exemplars of learners using the language, and host the results on the school's website or learning platform.
- Dovetail activities with national or international events, e.g. European Languages Day, the Olympics or the World Cup.

Teaching tip

Visit the Newbury Park website, which has a wealth of resources to introduce staff and children to the idea of 'Language of the month' and to showcase different ideas of possible activities (www.newburyparkschool.net/langofmonth/index.html).

Bonus idea ★

Use technology to trigger audio and video clips of children using their different languages, e.g. QR codes can be placed around the school, ready to play media clips when scanned with the camera on a phone or tablet device. In a similar way, mobile devices can access augmented technologies like *Aurasma,* which can overlay real objects with a video of a child talking.

Capitalise on the yearly events calendar

'We always make the most of national and international events to enrich the curriculum. It's a great way to involve our parents as well.'

Throughout the year, there are numerous religious, social and political events that can be woven into the curriculum.

Religious festivals occur throughout the year and provide a starting point for promoting and celebrating religious and cultural understanding. Other events provide natural opportunities to tackle difficult and complex issues. For example, January has *Holocaust Memorial Day*. In June, there is the potential to discuss issues of migration and asylum through *Gypsy Roma Traveller History Month* and *Refugee Week*. The *European Day of Languages* occurs in September every year and offers lots of opportunities for celebrating language and culture across the world. October brings *Black History Month* and *Show Racism the Red Card* always has a fortnight of action during this month as well. Unicef also has a *Day for Change* each calendar year. Here is a list of websites with more details on events that you may like to consider:

- Holocaust Memorial Day: www.hmd.org.uk
- Gypsy Roma Traveller History Month: https://www.natt.org.uk
- Refugee Week: www.refugeeweek.org.uk
- Show Racism the Red Card: www.srtrc.org
- European Day of Languages: https://edl.ecml.at
- Unicef Day for Change: www.unicef.org.uk/fundraise/fundraise-in-your-community/at-school/day-for-change.

Bonus idea ★

Sign up for the Shap e-calendar, which details all the major religious festivals and celebrations (www.shapworkingparty.org.uk/calendar.html).

Understanding social and cultural norms

'I was mortified to find out that it's considered rude to pat a child from a Hindu background on their head.'

Taking the time to learn about social and cultural norms specific to certain cultures can help avoid potentially embarrassing situations.

Taking it further

Produce a handout for staff summarising some of these social and cultural norms. However, it is imperative that you check your facts and sources rigorously.

Simple adjustments to the way we interact with people and correctly interpreting body language and similar behaviours will greatly improve effectiveness in dealing with learners and their parents or carers.

Ideas about body image and personal space can vary across cultures:

- In some traditions, people stand much closer when they are communicating.
- Sometimes individuals don't like to be touched by people outside the family circle – in some cultures, the head is considered sacred.
- Some Muslim girls and women will not shake hands with members of the opposite gender outside their immediate family.
- Boys and girls from some cultures may be unwilling or refuse to undress in front of peers – this has implications for changing for PE.

Body language and interactions can sometimes be interpreted differently or appear rude:

- Pupils may avoid eye contact with adults who are speaking to them, since in some cultures this is a sign of respect.
- Some people will nod and smile copiously during conversation, but this does not imply that they have fully understood.

- Conventions for showing understanding or agreement can vary, so much so that sometimes a nod of the head can mean 'no' and a shake of the head can mean 'yes'.
- Some cultures consider a pointing finger, thumbs up or showing the soles of the feet to be rude.

Languages that rely heavily on tone to convey meaning can sound strange to an untrained ear:

- Ordinary conversation in an unfamiliar L1 might sound rather loud, abrupt or aggressive.
- Certain forms or conventions can make language seem more direct, e.g. the use of 'will', as opposed to 'should' or 'could', can make the user sound rather bossy. Nuances like this often unintentionally transfer over when a bilingual person uses English.

Bonus idea ★

Create a set of short video clips to illustrate the complexities around cultural appropriacy. The app *Silent Movie* is a perfect tool for producing short video clips with captions to explain what is happening on screen. The black-and-white movie effect, 1920s music and lack of narration is a perfect medium for depersonalising situations and adding appropriate humour to what is a potentially serious subject.

Using persona dolls

'When one of my class was called a pejorative name by a peer, the persona doll session really helped unpick the issues in a sensitive way.'

Persona dolls are realistic dolls that can be transformed into 'little people' by providing them with their own personalities. Skilled practitioners can identify opportune moments to 'invite' them into classrooms to facilitate non-threatening discussion around sensitive and thought-provoking issues. Young children quickly identify with the dolls to the extent that they may come to see them as small friends. As the children begin to empathise, they may feel happy, sad or excited for the doll; they may offer helpful suggestions and words of support for the worries and problems that the doll may present.

Taking it further

Consider attending official Persona Doll training in order to ensure the most effective results with this technique (http://personadoll.uk).

How to build the doll's persona

The 'persona' should be introduced during the session as naturally as possible. How much or little of this is revealed will vary, depending on the purpose of the session, the age of the participating children and whether or not the doll is to become a regular visitor to the classroom. Interaction with the doll should be like holding a real child, including pretending to listen to the doll's comments and recasting them to the children.

Develop an appropriate scenario in order to:

- explore different lifestyles and types of family structures, e.g. being from a Traveller background
- share life experiences, e.g. living abroad and moving from another country
- celebrate diversity, e.g. knowing other languages or having a different faith
- introduce special events, e.g. festivals and remembrance days
- address sensitive issues, e.g. trauma, disability, discrimination and racism.

To prepare, you need to:

- invent a realistic background, e.g. name, family structure, country of origin, ethnicity, knowledge of languages, religion
- source relevant photographs, e.g. family members, pets, home, famous places, places of worship
- collect appropriate artefacts or media, e.g. favourite toys, clothing, food, religious artefacts, maps, music
- bind the materials together in a suitable format, e.g. a suitcase, a photograph album, diary or scrapbook.

It is a good idea to have prepared a number of specific 'questions' to promote participation from the audience, while maintaining flexibility when responding to their contributions.

Bonus idea ★

Talking photo albums are perfect for building back stories. Not only can you include suitable imagery and realia, but you can also record relevant music and speech (in L1 as well as English). These could be played during the persona doll session for added authenticity.

Avoiding stereotype and tokenism

'I advise schools to ensure they don't just hold one-off cultural events as this can be seen as rather tokenistic.'

Infusing the whole curriculum with a truly intercultural dimension doesn't happen overnight. It can't be treated as a 'tick-box' exercise, where 'visiting' other countries or cultures only happens on special occasions. A whole-school focus requires the full commitment of all the staff and learners at the school, as well as that of the wider community.

Here are some simple suggestions:

- Plan topics or themes at specific times of the year to naturally coincide with festivals, holidays, etc., in order to seamlessly integrate them into the curriculum.
- Actively seek out opportunities for intercultural work right across the curriculum.
- Offer a balanced view when considering life in other countries, particularly those in the 'developing world', e.g. show images of high-tech city living alongside quieter, simpler village life.
- Think about use of language, and try to avoid references like 'they' or 'them' or 'this is how we do such-and-such'.
- Check that books and digital resources are routinely scrutinised for stereotype and bias.
- Ensure that relevant resource material is on display and in classrooms throughout the year, rather than being wheeled out just for 'special' days.
- Where possible, draw upon the linguistic and cultural knowledge of the experts – EAL learners and their parents or carers – for assemblies and celebration events, as well to directly support class-based learning.

Teaching tip

You don't always need to resort to tried-and-tested activities from one year to the next. Rather than researching China or making a lantern for Chinese New Year, consider asking the children to interview members of the local Chinese association. Usually representatives from community organisations will be more than willing to help out with this type of request.

Taking it further

Find out more about approaches to avoid in teaching as part of a wider *Teaching and Learning Race Equality Toolkit* here: www. universities-scotland. ac.uk/raceequalitytoolkit/ context/approaches-to-avoid.htm.

Developing community partnerships

Part 9

How our school works video

'As a parent of a newly-arrived child, I had so many questions because our education system is completely different. The school produced a video answering many of these questions and I really appreciated it being in my language as well.'

New-arrival families will appreciate information about their child's new school in as accessible a format as possible. Bear in mind that this may also help established families, as moving from one school phase to the next can raise all sorts of additional questions.

Try involving the whole school community in the production of a video to explain all the essential information. Where possible, get learners involved in planning, filming, editing and writing or recording the narration.

The specific contents of such a video will vary from school to school, and it can sometimes be difficult to predict which elements will or will not be helpful. Try interviewing a range of BAME children and adults to elicit what information would have been most useful in preparation for starting school. There will be common elements, whether the learner is British-born or newly arrived from abroad.

It may help to split the final video into different sections, so that families can access the bits that seem most relevant to them; any information that you deem essential can be marked as such. Once it is finished, you can put the video on the school's website or make it available as a DVD.

> **Bonus idea** ★
>
> Ask parents, bilingual practitioners and other bilingual professionals (Idea 11) to help with producing high-quality translations. Dub the video in those languages most significant to the school's context. With the help of adults, bilingual children themselves may be able to voice over the video.

Celebrate achievements beyond the school

'Although I knew Rahana spoke Sylheti at home, I had no idea she was studying Bengali at Saturday school until her mum mentioned it the other day.'

Many children have linguistic, cultural and religious experiences that rarely interface with school life unless robust efforts are taken to find out about them. There are clear benefits for pupils in terms of motivation and self-esteem when teachers credit children for these aspects of their lives.

Find out whether EAL learners are continuing to study L1 outside of school. For some, this may be an informal home-based approach, while for others it will be at weekend community-language classes. Certificates obtained through supplementary schools could be given out during celebration assemblies.

Celebrate the fact that some learners have deeply religious lives that put major time constraints on their home life; dealing with this situation usually requires significant discipline. They may study a holy book, regularly attend a place of worship or have experienced a rite of passage at a particular age. Older Muslim children may fast during Ramadan; this can be another opportunity to credit learners for their achievements, and the school will need to be sensitive to these notable events.

Ask learners what responsibilities they have at home, e.g. do they interpret information for parents or care for younger siblings and elderly relatives? Where these responsibilities are proportionate to the age of the learner, schools could consider developing flexible arrangements to support each learner's individual circumstances.

Teaching tip

It is vital to keep accurate records of this kind of information and ensure that all relevant staff are kept informed. Passing on these records at the point of transition will be hugely beneficial for the learners themselves as well as for the receiving school.

Bonus idea ★

It can be a good idea to visit a local supplementary school and observe a teaching session. This will forge new relationships and give you a better insight into the typical working practices of these schools. It will also help if you wanted to offer your own school as a centre at some future time.

Family learning events

'I never went into school with my first child. But once I went to a numeracy workshop, I learned so much and it gave me confidence to go in again.'

While parents from many cultural backgrounds are more than happy to get involved in their child's school, some parents can be harder to engage. Family learning serves many purposes. It can help with those harder-to-reach groups, reinforce school messages, explain current teaching methods and, perhaps most importantly, break down barriers between different communities.

Organising family learning events is an effective way to encourage greater participation from parents or carers. Invite the whole family to attend sessions where everyone learns together. You may wish to focus on parents/carers from a specific ethnic background, target families of new-arrival learners or promote community cohesion by inviting families from a variety of ethnic backgrounds (including white British). Don't give up if turnout is initially low. Word gets round, and participation tends to improve the more sessions you arrange (sharing food from other cultures also helps!).

Family learning events can be used to:

- Reinforce important messages about maintenance of L1.
- Provide information about the UK education system and how the school works.
- Give some ideas on how best to support with homework or reading with their child.
- Help parents/carers experience what school examinations are like.
- Explain how to keep children safe when using the internet.
- Orient the school's position on 'British Values' within the wider context of promoting community cohesion and fostering understanding.

Accessing resources within the local community

'One of our parents owns a local restaurant and we invited them in during international week to run a cooking masterclass for Year 5.'

Sometimes schools don't make enough use of the resource base that is available through the various ethnic, cultural and religious groups within the local community. Consider making this a core responsibility for a member of staff.

Most of the major BAME groups in the area will have an official association that represents them. If you are seeking information about the history and culture of a specific group, then this is a good starting point. Children from service families will have local contacts from within the Ministry of Defence who can provide advice and guidance for the particular needs of these children and their families.

Audit the area for shops, businesses and religious centres to get some useful contacts. Inviting successful role models from BAME communities to the school is a way of enriching the curriculum and helps with identifying potential speakers for assemblies. You may be able to identify suitable places for school visits in order to support the teaching of RE. New-arrival families will also really appreciate knowing where and when local supplementary language schools operate (Idea 87).

Knowing what services are on offer in the local authority will really benefit newly-arrived families. There may be specific local services for ethnic minority families with children and young adults with disabilities. Also, you may be able to recommend specific points of contact for children and young people from refugee or asylum-seeking families, e.g. legal services and charitable groups in the area.

Taking it further

Make contact with your local authority as they will certainly have lists of organisations that cater for the distinctive needs of children and families from BAME communities.

Early language development and maintenance of L1

'Should we stop using our language at home and only talk in English?'

Natural exposure to more than one spoken language as a child grows up is very common across the world. Research unequivocally supports the benefits of a multilingual upbringing.

Talk with parents or carers as soon as an EAL child starts school, and reinforce the school's position on early language development and the importance of maintaining L1. This will be important not only for the pupil but also for younger siblings who may not yet be in school. Should the child go on to develop literacy in more than one language, then hearing and learning to talk in those languages is obviously beneficial. This is as important for British-born children as for those who are new arrivals.

Some families have lost the art of using songs and rhymes to engage their children. You may find it useful to initiate a family learning session (Idea 88) to introduce parents or carers to traditional English-language songs and nursery rhymes, and it may be useful to elicit examples from their own cultural background. Try recording songs or rhymes from Britain and other countries onto a CD and loan it out to families with young children.

Explain the importance of exposing children to bilingual print from an early age. Direct parents or carers to local sources such as road and shop signs, menus, food labels and newspapers. Encourage them to read to their children from bilingual texts, and get them to make reference to both language scripts so that their children become familiar with the written form of the languages that they are hearing or learning as they grow up.

Activities for learners who take extended visits

'Sarfraz enjoyed telling us all about his trip home to Pakistan. I learned a lot and it was very enriching for the rest of his class.'

Rather than making it a problem when children take extended visits, practitioners should treat it as a learning opportunity.

Here are some ideas for supporting learners when they make extended visits away from school:

- Develop procedures that enable pupils to continue their studies while on their trip.
- Provide learners with a disposable camera so they can take pictures of their activities.
- Where possible, entrust learners with digital media equipment to take pictures or record sounds.
- Encourage learners to keep a diary of their trip.
- Suggest that learners collect interesting resources to show classmates on their return, such as food labels, menus, newspapers, toys, musical instruments, games and the like.

When learners return, they could share their experience:

- by performing a show-and-tell for their classmates about some aspect of their trip
- by contributing to an assembly about their country or cultural background
- by making a talking book (Idea 44) about their time away.

Bonus idea

Develop your own booklet/pack for children who are making an extended visit abroad. A good example can be found here: Extended Holiday workbook Key Stage 2 – Milton Keynes Council (www.milton-keynes.gov.uk/assets/attach/8868/Final-ks2-ext-break.pdf).

Videoconferencing (VC)

'We felt Sundai was very isolated because no one in school could speak Shona. However, we set her up on a VC link with another child from Zimbabwe and it really helped her settle.'

Videoconferencing is an essential tool for communication at a distance – locally, nationally and even internationally.

Teaching tip

Check out some of the free tools that are available for videoconferencing, such as *FlashMeeting, Skype* and *Google+ Hangouts*.

VC is perfect for learning languages in general because it enables speakers of other languages to practise their oral skills by developing questioning and interview skills in the target language – in this case English. When learners from similar and different backgrounds can socialise together or work on curriculum-related projects within any subject area, community cohesion is enhanced. Experts from BAME communities can be 'invited' into the classroom to share skills and experiences and act as positive role models. Practitioners can also use VC to liaise together and develop their expertise in managing ethnic-minority achievement.

Planning for a VC session:

- Book a quiet room or area for the session.
- Ensure that all the equipment is working.
- Check that the VC client works; some local authorities block certain software.
- Ensure that when learners are communicating together, they are always supervised by an adult.
- Note that some VC software allows users to record the session for playback at a later date; while this can be very useful, it is important to check parental permissions when children and young people are involved.

Here are a few ideas for videoconferencing:

1. **Linking isolated EAL learners.** Many schools have relatively small numbers of BAME learners, and often their EAL population

tends to be culturally and linguistically isolated; this can also be true of their families. Try to identify same-language speakers in other isolated situations in order to facilitate communication through a VC link. This allows EAL learners the opportunity to practise L1 and socialise with those of a similar age and background.

2. **Community cohesion projects – linking learners from mainly white schools with those from ethnically diverse settings (and vice versa).** This is a useful way of enabling white British pupils to meet and interact with learners with whom they would not normally have contact because of the locality of their school or home. In this way, individuals and groups can socialise together or take part in more structured activities that look at the commonality and differences between people. It can be a useful way to prepare for learner-exchange visits and can also facilitate follow-up work.

3. **Bilingual Q&A sessions for parents of new arrivals.** Organising events where a bilingual practitioner is at the end of a VC link at a pre-arranged time can be useful to enable parents to ask questions in L1 about education and other related matters. This will help not only their school-aged children but also older siblings in terms of signposting them on to further education.

4. **Bilingual storytelling.** One practitioner can efficiently deliver a bilingual storytelling session to lots of learners in different schools. This will help raise the self-esteem of EAL learners who know the same language because they can become experts for the day. Besides supporting language learning and contributing to the intercultural dimension of the curriculum, it will also be enriching for monolingual learners.

Teaching tip

You could also try an 'Ask the experts' session by inviting members of local BAME community groups to become experts for the day. Using VC technology, the 'experts' can enter classrooms virtually to talk about lifestyle or to showcase their own expertise in work, religious practice or a creative talent. Try linking this with special celebrations or national or international events (Idea 82).

School-linking projects

'Our children can't wait to receive a termly letter from our partner school in Kenya. It really helps our children understand what it means to live in another country.'

There can be many benefits from linking with schools locally, nationally or even internationally. Having educational links with a diverse range of schools provides opportunities to support community cohesion and develop a culturally-infused curriculum.

Taking it further

Register with the British Council's *Schools Online* website to start your journey along the way to finding a partner school and accessing core professional development opportunities (https://schoolsonline.britishcouncil.org).

How and when you decide to initiate linking projects will depend on the specific character of your school. Generally, contact starts through a series of email exchanges, although communication can be enhanced through videoconferencing (Idea 92). You may decide to run projects in out-of-hours settings so that learners can communicate in a fairly informal way. Alternatively, projects can be tied more directly to the curriculum. Try developing projects that require learners to compare and contrast locality, history or lifestyle.

Successful school-linking projects frequently lead to learner exchanges and all the learning opportunities that these entail. Exchanges potentially include: significant moments in a learner's life such as the first time visiting a city, the countryside or the coast; the opportunity to socialise with someone from a different ethnicity or religious tradition; the first visit to another country. There is opportunity here to exchange art works or musical compositions or to initiate joint writing projects. Make a point of creating activities that challenge learners' perceptions of the world around them. Also, where possible, encourage learners to communicate through shared languages, as this enables EAL learners to practise L1 and supports the overall delivery of languages across the school.

Whole-school approaches

Part 10

Organising provision

'All schools will benefit from a senior manager who leads on ethnic minority achievement (EMA).'

Experience shows that this is an area of provision that necessarily involves the whole school community. Many schools, particularly those with significant numbers of BAME learners, build a team of practitioners to work with new arrivals, help deliver intervention sessions and support classroom practitioners in developing sound EAL practice.

Taking it further

Check out these resources for very comprehensive guidance around practice and provision for EAL learners: www.naldic.org.uk/eal-teaching-and-learning/outline-guidance; DCSF (2009) 'Ensuring the Attainment of More Advanced Learners of English as an Additional Language (EAL)'; DCSF (2007) 'New Arrivals Excellence Programme: Guidance (Primary)'; and DfES (2006) 'Excellence and Enjoyment: Learning and Teaching for Bilingual Children in the Primary Years'.

Here are some specific tasks for anyone who has recently inherited this role or is looking to develop it further:

- Clearly identify roles and responsibilities within the school so that the key tasks do not fall upon the shoulders of just one person.
- Develop a specific policy for EAL (Idea 95) and/or ensure that references to EAL are made within all relevant policies: teaching and learning, inclusion, assessment, etc.
- Audit the school population and ensure that the data captures ethnicity, date of birth, date of arrival in the UK, L1, religion, country of origin and other essential information (Idea 3).
- Implement an EAL-friendly assessment framework (Idea 14).
- Develop tracking systems to monitor both attainment and progress of BAME and EAL learners, making comparisons between different ethnic groups and the WBRI population, as well as identifying the rate of progress for any individual learner.
- Establish an ongoing programme of CPD (Idea 99) for all the staff in school, focusing on strategies to support beginner and advanced learners and promoting cultural diversity through the curriculum and race-equality training (including reporting and recording racist incidents).

Develop an EAL policy

'When I looked on the website, I was really encouraged to see that they had an up-to-date EAL policy.'

All schools should have an EAL policy, whether they actually have EAL pupils attending the school or not.

It is best practice that any EAL policy sits within or alongside the equality policy. An EAL policy should articulate how the school will:

- Provide a safe and secure learning environment for all EAL pupils, supporting them to become independent learners.
- Ensure there is enough curriculum support to help learners to make excellent progress.
- Group EAL learners by academic potential rather than English language proficiency.
- Aspire for high expectations and achievement for all.
- Develop links with parents and communities.

The policy should also clarify how the school will provide:

- in-depth assessment of the needs of new-arrival EAL learners
- in-class support for EAL pupils
- high-quality English language teaching
- training that develops subject teachers' competence in meeting the linguistic and learning needs of bilingual pupils in the mainstream
- appropriate curriculum, teaching strategies and resources
- monitoring and evaluation of teaching programmes and pupil progress and attainment.

The policy should have a review date and specify which senior manager is responsible for keeping the policy up to date.

Taking it further

A school may not necessarily require an EAL policy if other relevant policies are infused by appropriate statements, e.g. equality, assessment, teaching and learning, etc. Threading comments throughout other policies suggests a more integrated approach to practice and provision for EAL learners than having a stand-alone policy.

Bonus idea ★

The EAL policy should also clarify the school's language and literacy policy with regard to how EAL learners can use their existing language abilities and knowledge in different contexts, and for different purposes around the school, as well as meet new language in contexts that are familiar and supportive.

Conduct a learning environment walk

'It was very revealing to walk around the school with a parent and see everything through their eyes.'

Experience suggests that a learning environment audit is best performed by two or more practitioners — perhaps a senior leader and a governor with responsibility for inclusion. It is also an activity that could involve BAME parents and the school council.

Taking it further

It's also worth taking a virtual tour of the school's online presence — the public-facing website, as well as any social media accounts. How accessible would information and linked documents be to families from BAME backgrounds? What additional measures could be implemented to alleviate any potential barriers?

Bonus idea ★

Consider whether the phone system presents a barrier to communication. Even when the school has a low percentage of BAME/EAL learners, this is still an important consideration.

How welcoming does the school feel to people from BAME backgrounds? This is important, because the learning environment communicates something about the school's attitude towards inclusion in its widest sense.

The school office is often the first point of contact for many families and a good place to start the 'walk'. What is your immediate impression as you enter this area? Are there dual-language welcome signs? Does the library stock a good range of dual-language dictionaries, bilingual books and stories from other cultures? Are materials routinely checked to avoid stereotype and/or tokenism? What about the corridors, classrooms and other school areas? Ideally, you should see intercultural displays that demonstrate the school's commitment to developing a culturally infused curriculum, with examples of work from BAME/EAL as well as non-EAL learners. Dual-language material that celebrates the many languages of famous people that are also used within the school community should be visible, as should photographs of people drawn from a range of ethnic backgrounds, role-play/display areas that contain artefacts sourced from a range of religious and cultural contexts.

Running the Young Interpreter Scheme®

'I got picked to be a Young Interpreter because I have lots of different qualities: I speak several languages but I am also a good listener and enjoy helping people.'

The Young Interpreter Scheme® capitalises on the huge potential within each school to use the linguistic and social skills of all their learners to support the development of an inclusive and welcoming environment for EAL learners and their families.

The scheme is most effective when bilingual learners are trained alongside non-EAL pupils. Confident bilingual pupils learn how to utilise their L1 skills when working with beginner EAL learners, particularly new arrivals. English-only speakers work alongside them to employ strategies and resources for giving support in situations where an L1 is not shared between pupils and adults.

The scheme goes way beyond arranging peer buddies (Idea 7) for new-arrival EAL learners. Potential activities permeate the whole school, from promoting cultural and linguistic diversity to supporting individual EAL learners and families in and out of the classroom.

Potential activities can include the following:

- Showing visitors and new-arrival families around the school.
- Spending break times with new arrivals.
- Inducting and settling new learners, including familiarising them with school systems.
- Using interpreting skills to facilitate informal home–school communication.
- Supporting peers in the classroom with routine activities.
- Offering taster language sessions for peers and school staff.

Teaching tip

Young Interpreters should not be used as a replacement for professional adult interpreters, nor should they get significantly involved in translation work. Further guidance about this issue can be accessed here: http://www3.hants. gov.uk/education/emtas/ supportinglanguages/ pupilinterpreters.htm.

Taking it further

The official Young Interpreter Scheme® has infant, junior and secondary versions and all the training materials can be accessed online. Find out more here: http://www3.hants.gov. uk/education/emtas-2/ goodpractice-2/hyis.htm. Alternatively, you can follow them on Twitter @YIscheme and on Facebook (www.facebook. com/Young-Interpreter-Scheme-1393344670884345).

TalkingPartners@Primary and Talking Maths

'We have found a rigorous focus on peer talk has transformed standards across the school.'

If you are looking for a way to initiate a whole-school focus on speaking and listening, then you might want to consider implementing TalkingPartners@Primary and/or Talking Maths; these are highly successful programmes that are based on a tried-and-tested model of talk-based intervention for beginner EAL learners.

Taking it further

Any school wishing to implement either of these programmes should send one or more lead practitioners to a training event, where they will also receive a comprehensive set of support materials. A key manager should also oversee the running of these programmes. Over time, schools will benefit from cascading training down to other staff and incorporating the approaches back into the mainstream curriculum, thereby developing a whole-school emphasis on speaking and listening. Visit www.educationworks.org.uk/what-we-do/speaking-and-listening/talkingpartnersprimary and www.educationworks.org.uk/what-we-do/mathematics/talking-maths for more details.

TalkingPartners@Primary is a short-term intervention aimed at boosting oral skills for targeted pupils in order to produce confident and independent learners. Led by a trained practitioner, the sessions are based around practical, collaborative games and activities, where speaking and listening are central to learning. Effective modelling by the lead practitioner is key to success, and planning between the facilitator and class teacher ensures that the content of each session is linked directly to the mainstream curriculum. Run over ten weeks, one practitioner works with three learners for three sessions per week. Each session is oral, starting with a five-minute warm-up followed by a specific focus. Throughout each session, the facilitator keeps detailed notes about each child's progress on a range of indicators.

Talking Maths is organised similarly to TalkingPartners@Primary. With an emphasis on speaking and listening, it uses games and activities to focus on the understanding and use of mathematical language. It enables learners to be more precise in their use of language to explain and justify their mathematical thinking and has been shown to raise their participation levels in mainstream classes.

Continuing professional development (CPD)

'Regularly meeting EAL professionals at networking meetings has given me so much confidence as the EAL coordinator at my school.'

All staff need access to high-quality CPD, as pedagogy and resourcing inevitably change and develop over time. This can be anything from face-to-face training and access to eLearning, to attending different types of network meetings and even more formalised accredited training.

Finding advice and guidance can sometimes be difficult, and you may need to do some research into what resources are available (locally or online). Here are some starting points:

- Join NALDIC – National Association for Language Development in the Curriculum. Membership benefits include full access to their website, free copies of the *EAL Journal* (a termly magazine of practice, research and activism) and discounts on annual conference fees.
- SATEAL is the EAL professional body for Scotland (www.sateal.org.uk), NASSEA is the professional hub for the EMA practitioners in North of England (http://nassea.org.uk) and EALAW is the EAL professional body for Wales (www.ealaw.org.uk/index.php/about-ealaw).
- Look out for networks of professionals that meet from time to time in and around your area. TeachMeets sometimes have a focus on EAL, and NALDIC supports Regional Interest Groups (RIGs) all over the country.
- Check out what's available online, as universities, NGOs (non-governmental organisations) and charities sometimes offer free EAL CPD.
- Connect with relevant organisations on Facebook and Twitter (see @EAL_naldic on Twitter to get you started).

Taking it further

Join EAL-Bilingual, an online professional e-mail network for all things connected with EAL and bilingual teaching and learning. You can join here: https://groups.google.com/forum/#!forum/eal-bilingual.

Bonus idea ★

Many universities run masters-level accredited face-to face or distance learning courses connected with bilingual education/EAL matters. While this can be professionally developing for any school-based practitioner, it may be essential for an EMA coordinator or to become an EAL adviser within a local authority. For information, visit https://naldic.org.uk/professional-learning-cpd.

Six of the best from the internet

'Joining NALDIC has been the most useful step I have taken all year.'

The EAL community is very close-knit and there's always someone online who is prepared to offer free support and guidance.

Teaching tip

It is worth researching useful sites around the internet, and obviously the search term 'English as an additional language' (encapsulated in quotation marks) will find many of them. However, bilingual education is an issue that affects many other localities, which use different terms for the same issue, e.g. Canada and USA: English Language Learners and Australia: English as an additional language or Dialect. While English as a second language (ESL) is not synonymous with EAL, you may find useful resources using that term as well.

1. National Association for Language Development in the Curriculum (NALDIC)
www.naldic.org.uk

This is one of the most comprehensive websites around, offering a good balance between theoretical research and practical teaching and learning pedagogy. While there is a lot of open access material, the majority of the downloadable articles, documents and media clips only become available upon payment of an annual membership fee.

2. The EAL MESHGuide
www.meshguides.org/guides/node/112

As stated on the website, *'This guide is written principally to support teachers and learning support assistants working with EAL learners in any educational setting and who are at any stage of fluency in the learning of English. It will also support senior leaders in their strategic response to the EAL learners in their schools. As with all MESHGuides, it seeks to share knowledge with professionals in order to support the growth of evidence informed practice that works in promoting the best in pupil outcomes'.*

3. EAL Nexus Project
https://ealresources.bell-foundation.org.uk

A partnership between The British Council and The Bell Foundation, this website is a single point of contact for EAL resourcing and pedagogy. As well as information pages and downloadable resources, there are also some interesting research reports and video case studies.

4. The Collaborative Learning Project
www.collaborativelearning.org

Many sites offer downloadable teaching materials; one of the best is the Collaborative Learning Project, which hosts activities created by teachers for teachers. Developed over many years, the site is a cornucopia of downloadable activities aimed at developing the oral skills of EAL learners.

5. EMTAS4Success (a local authority website)
www.sgsts.org.uk/SupportForVulnerablePupils/EMTAS/SitePages/Home.aspx

It's worth doing a search for relevant local-authority websites around the United Kingdom. An internet search for keywords like 'ethnic minority achievement service' will find most of them. There are many notable sites, but EMTAS4Success is a particularly rich resource with many downloadable guidance documents.

6. Hampshire Ethnic Minority Achievement Service (EMTAS) – online EAL eLearning
http://emtas.hias.hants.gov.uk/course/view.php?id=19

The Hampshire EMTAS EAL eLearning involves interactive online training units that cater for the needs of EAL learners, aimed at teachers, TAs, inclusion managers and governors, with particular relevance for NQTs and trainee teachers. Each unit is self-certificated upon completion. Topics covered include: 'bilingualism', 'working with parents', 'SEND:EAL interface', 'culturally inclusive school' and 'teaching and learning', among many others.

Bonus idea ★

Look out for free information, resources and training events via your teaching union association.

References and further reading

Cameron, L. (2002). 'Measuring vocabulary size in English as an additional language', *Language Teaching Research*, 6(2) 145–173.

Cameron, L. (2003). *Writing in English as an Additional Language at Key Stage 4 and Post-16*. London: Ofsted. Available at: www.naldic.org.uk/research-and-information/research+summaries/cameron.html.

Cummins J. (2011). *Identity Texts*. London: Trentham Books.

DCSF (2007). *New Arrivals Excellence Programme: Guidance (Primary)*. London: DCSF.

DCSF (2009). *Ensuring the Attainment of More Advanced Learners of EAL*. London: DfES.

DfES (2002) Grammar for Writing: Supporting pupils learning EAL'. Available at: http://www.naldic.org.uk/Resources/NALDIC/Teaching%20and%20Learning/ealgrammar.pdf.

DfES (2006). *Excellence and Enjoyment: Learning and Teaching for Bilingual Children in the Primary Years.* London: DfES.

Fisher Family Trust. 'Student explorer'. Available at: https://fft.org.uk/fft/student-explorer/.

Gibbons, P. (1991). *Learning to Learn in a Second Language*. Australia: PETA.

Gibbons, P. (2008). 'Challenging pedagogies: more than just good practice?'. *NALDIC Quarterly*, 6(2) 4–14.

Jewitt, C. & Kress, G. (Eds.) (2003). *Multimodal Literacy*. New York: Peter Lang.

Krashen, S. D. (1982). 'Principles and practice of second language acquisition'. Available at: http://www.sdkrashen.com/content/books/principles_and_practice.pdf.

Krathwohl, D. R. (2002). 'A revision of Bloom's taxonomy: an overview'. *Theory into Practice*, 41(4) 212–218.

Pim, C. (2017). *Developing the Writing of Advanced EAL Learners through the Use of 3D Immersive Adventure Games*. EAL Nexus Research Project. British Council.

Vygotsky, L. S. (1978). *Mind and Society: The Development of Higher Psychological Processes*. Cambridge, MA: Harvard University Press.